Interference Control
in Computers
and Microprocessor-Based
Equipment

by
Michel Mardiguian

Don White Consultants, Inc.
Gainesville, Virginia USA

First Edition
Sixth Printing 1989

Interference Control Technologies
Don White Consultants Inc. Subsidiary
State Route 625, P.O. Box D
Gainesville, Virginia 22065 USA
Telephone (703) 347-0030   Telex 89-9165 DWCI GAIV

Library of Congress Catalog Card No. 84-172962
ISBN 0-932263-23-2

Printed in the United States of America

D
621·3819'58
MAR

Preface

I would like to express my sincere thanks to the people who, through their advice, assistance, and careful workmanship made this book come to life. First, thank you, Edward Price, Chief Editor and Production Manager at Don White Consultants, and your team, for the fine work and meticulous handling of the drafting, typesetting, design and publication.

Also I thank the EMC Engineers at the Philips Company in Sweden for their careful and constructive technical review. I am also grateful to Ulf Nilsson, my colleague at DWCI who provided many useful comments.

In addition, I would especially like to dedicate this book to three people who played important roles in my career. The first person is my father, an electrician with a modest educational background but a great *sixth sense* , who gave me my first *taste* of experimenting with electricity. The second person is Ralph Calcavecchio, of the IBM Kingston Research Laboratory, who was my teacher and inspiration while I was with IBM France, and whose scientific attitude and constant search for engineering excellence was a model for many of us. Last, and not the least, is Donald R.J. White to whom I think all EMC engineers are indebted one way or another. At a time when we were fighting with the *jigsaw puzzle* of multi-system EMI, he developed the sound and orderly methodology for putting the pieces together.

March 1984   Michel Mardiguian
Gainesville, Virginia

Handbooks Published by ICT

(1) Carstensen, Russell V., *EMI Control in Boats and Ships,* 1979.

(2) Denny, Hugh W., *Grounding for Control of EMI,* 1983.

(3) Duff, Dr. William G., *A Handbook on Mobile Communications,* 1980.

(4) Duff, Dr. William G. and White, Donald R.J., Volume 5, *Electromagnetic Interference Prediction & Analysis Techniques,* 1972.

(5) Gabrielson, Bruce C., *The Aerospace Engineer's Handbook of Lightning Protection,* 1987.

(6) Gard, Michael F., *Electromagnetic Interference Control in Medical Electronics,* 1979.

(7) Georgopoulos, Dr. Chris J., *Fiber Optics and Optical Isolators,* 1982.

(8) Georgopoulos, Dr. Chris J., *Interference Control in Cable and Device Interfaces,* 1987.

(9) Ghose, Rabindra N., *EMP Environment and System Hardness Design,* 1983.

(10) Hart, William C. and Malone, Edgar W., *Lightning and Lightning Protection,* 1979.

(11) Hill, James S. and White, Donald R.J., Volume 6, *Electromagnetic Interference Specifications, Standards & Regulations,* 1975.

(12) Jansky, Donald M., *Spectrum Management Techniques,* 1977.

(13) Mardiguian, Michel, *Interference Control in Computers and Microprocessor-Based Equipment,* 1984.

(14) Mardiguian, Michel, *Electrostatic Discharge—Understand, Simulate and Fix ESD Problems,* 1985.

(15) Mardiguian, Michel, *How to Control Electrical Noise,* 1983.

(16) Smith, Albert A., *Coupling of External Electromagnetic Fields to Transmission Lines,* 1986.

(17) White, Donald R.J., *A Handbook on Electromagnetic Shielding Materials and Performance,* 1980.

(18) White, Donald R.J., *Electrical Filters—Synthesis, Design & Applications,* 1980.

(19) White, Donald R.J., *EMI Control in the Design of Printed Circuit Boards and Backplanes,* 1982. (Also available in French.)

(20) White, Donald R.J., *EMI Control Methodology & Procedures,* 1982.

(21) White, Donald R.J., Volume 1, *Electrical Noise and EMI Specifications,* 1971.

(22) White, Donald R.J., Volume 2, *Electromagnetic Interference Test Methods and Procedures,* 1980.

(23) White, Donald, R.J., Volume 3, *Electromagnetic Interference Control Methods & Techniques,* 1973.

(24) White, Donald R.J., Volume 4, *Electromagnetic Interference Test Instrumentation Systems,* 1980.

(25) White, Donald R.J., *Shielding Design Methodology and Procedures,* 1986.

(26) *EMC Technology 1982 Anthology*

Notice

All of the books listed above are available for purchase from Interference Control Technologies, Inc., Don White Consultants, Subsidiary, State Route 625, P.O. Box D, Gainesville, Virginia 22065 USA. Telephone: (703) 347-0030; Telex: 89-9165 DWCI GAIV. For countries outside North America, contact Els de Groot, ICT, Holland, Kerkstraat 63-65, 2355 AH Hoogmade, Holland. Telephone (31) 1712 2526; Telex 844-30268.

Table of Contents

Interference Control in Computers and Microprocessor-Based Equipment

Page No.

Preface   i
Other Books Published by DWCI   ii
Table of Contents   iii
Introduction   v

Chapter 1   Generalities on EMI and Noise Coupling   1.1

1.1   The Threat from Electromagnetics   1.1
1.2   Outside Sources of EMI and Their Remedies   1.5
               1.2.1 CW Transmitters   1.5
               1.2.2 High Frequency (Other Than Radio) Generators   1.6
               1.2.3 Broadband/Transient Sources   1.6
               1.2.4 Lightning   1.7
               1.2.5 Electrostatic Discharge   1.7
               1.2.6 Power Line Disturbances   1.8
               Summary   1.9

Chapter 2   PCB Design and Layout   2.1

2.1   Components Properties Regarding Noise   2.1
               2.1.1 The Problem of Analog Circuits   2.1
               2.1.2 Some Logic Families   2.3
2.2   Printed Circuit Board: The First Building Block   2.6
               2.2.1 Voltage Distribution and Zero-Volt Return   2.6
                      2.2.1.1 Decoupling   2.6
                      2.2.1.2 Other Methods of Voltage Distribution Clean-Up   2.10
               2.2.2 Analog/Digital Mix   2.14
2.3   Physical Implementation and Zoning   2.17
               2.3.1 Wirewrap, Single Layer Board   2.17
               2.3.2 Single Layer PC Boards   2.20
               2.3.3 The Ultimate Answer to PCB Noise Suppression—
               Multilayer Boards   2.23
               2.3.4 Multi-Wire Boards   2.27
               2.3.5 Reciprocity Between Susceptibility and Emission   2.28
               Summary   2.31

Chapter 3   Motherboard Design and Layout   3.1
3.1   Crosstalk Between Traces   3.2
3.2   Impedance Matching   3.5
3.3   Connector Areas at Motherboard Interface   3.5
               Summary   3.9

Chapter 4   **Power Supplies**   **4.1**
4.1   Packaging   4.1
4.2   Filtering and Shielding at the Power Supply Level   4.4
    Summary   4.6

Chapter 5   **Internal Wiring and Packaging**   **5.1**
5.1   Routing   5.1
5.2   EMI Protection of Logic/Signal Cabling Category (3)   5.2
5.3   Impedance of Discrete Wires and Jumpers   5.6
5.4   Grounding Scheme   5.8
    Summary   5.10

Chapter 6   **Final Box Design**   **6.1**
6.1   Main Housing: The Outer Barrier Against EMI   6.1
6.2   Shielding with Covers and Panels Seams   6.5
       6.2.1   Cover Material   6.5
       6.2.2   Cover Packaging   6.6
       6.2.3   Covers-to-Main Frame Bonding   6.6
6.3   Interface with Power Mains   6.9
       6.3.1   Selecting the Right Mains Filter   6.9
       6.3.2   Low Cost Filters   6.10
       6.3.3   Filter Location   6.11
       6.3.4   Transient Suppressors Other than Filters   6.13
       6.3.5   Shielding of AC Cables   6.14
6.4   Penetration and Immunization of Signal Interface Cables   6.15
       6.4.1   Special Types of Filtering for I/O Signal Cables   6.17
       6.4.2   Improving Cabling Immunity to EMI   6.20
6.5   Specially Hardened Equipment Housing   6.22
    Summary   6.25

Chapter 7   **Testing**   **7.1**
7.1   Emission Testing   7.1
7.2   Computers Emission Limits in the USA   7.4
7.3   Susceptibility Testing   7.5
7.4   Military Standards   7.6

Chapter 8   **Conclusion**   **8.1**

Appendix A   **A.1**
Appendix B   **B.1**
Appendix C   **C.1**
Appendix D   **D.1**
Appendix E   **E.1**
Appendix F   **F.1**

Glossary and Abbreviations   **G.1**

Bibliography   **H.1**

Introduction

Electromagnetic Interference, like vibration, acoustics or climatic conditions, is a significant part of the overall environment and strongly affects the performance of electronic equipment and devices. In turn the devices themselves contribute to the budget of electromagnetic effects. Coping with this phenomenon is often considered to be the domain of highly specialized individuals and therefore is not taken into account during the initial design stages; instead, the resultant test data are awaited "to see if it passes."

This situation is regrettable, especially in the computer industry. Logic designers do not often realize that when digital pulses with transition times of nanoseconds or less are used, all sorts of associated problems of radiation, parasitic couplings, etc., occur and every trace becomes an efficient radiating or receiving antenna.

This manual does not pretend to transform a reader into an EMC engineer, but it will permit a person to avoid most of the classical EMI pitfalls in his first design attempt. Even if some problems remain, they should be relatively few and easier for an EMI specialist to solve.

1 Generalities on EMI and Noise Coupling

Whenever an electronic device or a piece of electronic equipment creates electrical noise that interferes with the performance of other electrical equipment, or whenever a device is adversely affected by an external noise source, *Electromagnetic Interference (EMI)* is present. Examples of EMI include such events as: scratchy noises on Hi-Fi speakers when an electrical switch is activated or by an operating vacuum cleaner; disruption of TV reception by amateur radio transceivers; and noisy telephones resulting from transients caused by lightning. Static discharges between people and equipment, particularly during dry seasons, can severely affect computers. Other significant examples are when industrial remote-control devices are inadvertently triggered by an electric welding machine, or when the auto-pilot of an aircraft if jammed by a ground based transmitter.

1.1 The Threat from Electromagnetics

The ever increasing number of electronic devices using compact sensitive, or high-speed components, make the incidents of interference more frequent, particularly as new circuits become more miniaturized and equipment more compact. All such EMI phenomena can be clearly understood by a single common denominator they all share, i.e.,the *source to victim* concept (see Fig. 1.1).

When there is an EMI problem, there is always a noise *source* and a *victim* (device) where the trouble or problem is occurring.

In order for a noise source to cause interference, there *MUST BE A COUPLING PATH* between the source and victim. It is obvious, therefore, that interference can be reduced, without introducing sophisticated mathematics, at one or more of the following levels: following levels:

- *SOURCE*—by decoupling, shielding, or simply making a noiseless design.
- *COUPLING PATH*—by spacing or shielding if the coupling path is radiation, or filtering if the coupling path is conduction.

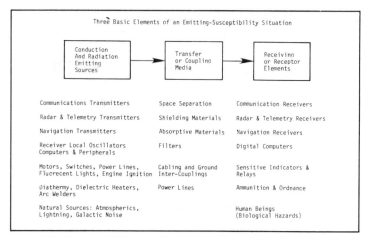

Figure 1.1—Three Basic Elements of an Emitting/Susceptibility Situation.

- *VICTIM*—by local decoupling, isolating, shielding or by circuit redesign using less susceptible components.

Now, consider the numerical values involved (GETTING AWAY FROM THE DECIBEL'S NIGHTMARE). To evaluate the amount of noise reduction provided by a *filter* or a *shield,* the expression is exactly like the one used by electricians for a voltage or current gain, i.e.,

$$20 \log_{10} \left(\frac{V_{out}}{V_{in}} \right) \tag{1.1}$$

except, in this case, noise reduction is of primary interest (not noise gain). For instance, in Fig. 1.2, the spike created by the electrical switch arcing is reduced by a small filter on the power input of the Hi-Fi tuner, which has a ratio of 200 volts/2 volts = 100 or 40 dB attenuation. Table 1.1 gives the significance of decibel as a ratio.

Similarly, a shield which attenuates an unwanted field by a factor of 10 is a barrier with 20 dB shielding effectiveness. In all cases, this is a ratio of Volts/Volts, i.e., a *dimensionless number.*

As a general rule, the attenuation effectiveness in terms of dB values can be grouped as follows:

- 0 to 10 dB = Poor attenuation, a filter which reduces the conducted noise (or a shield reducing the EMI field) by this amount hardly pays for itself. The effect may be noticeable, but it cannot be relied upon to eliminate EMI.

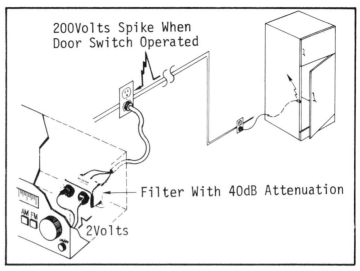

Fig. 1.2—Illustration of the Attenuation of a Filter.

Table 1.1—The Decibel as a Ratio

$\text{Voltage Ratio} = 20 \log_{10}\left(\dfrac{V_1}{V_2}\right)$			$\text{Power Ratio} = 10 \log_{10}\left(\dfrac{P_1}{P_2}\right)$		
dB	Power Ratio	Voltage Ratio	dB	Power Ratio	Voltage Ratio
0	1.00	1.00	10	10	3.16
1	1.26	1.12	20	100	10
3	2.00	1.41	30	1k	31.6
5	3.16	1.78	60	1M	1000
6	≈4.00	2.00	− 10	.1	.316
7	5.00	2.24	− 20	.01	.10
9	≈8.00	2.82	− 30	.001	.0316
10	10.00	3.16	− 60	10^{-6}	.001

- 10 to 30 dB = minimum range for achieving meaningful attenuation. In mild cases, EMI would be eliminated.

- 30 to 60 dB = range where the average EMI problems can be solved.

- over 60 dB = range for gaining above average attenuation—requires special attention and quality in shield and/or filter mountings (surface preparation, gasketing, bonding, etc.). Reserved for equipment which must operate at, or near, a 100% dependability factor and in extreme environments.

In expressing the amplitude of a noise voltage (when EMI is conducted), or the electromagnetic field which is creating noise, EMI specialists seldom use the terms Volt, or Volt/meter. Instead, they use equivalent values in decibels, which means that a noise voltage of 10 volts is expressed as: $20 \log_{10}(10)$ decibels above 1 Volt, or 20 dB Volt, since $\log_{10}$ of $10 = 1$.

Very low noise levels involved in EMI require the use of a smaller unit than the volt, i.e., the microvolt (μV). Similarly, a noise amplitude of 100μV, for instance, is expressed as $20 \log_{10} (100\mu$V), i.e., $20 \log_{10}(100)$ decibels above one μVolt. Therefore, 100 μV is equivalent to 40 dBμV. An electromagnetic field strength of 1 mV/meter, i.e., 1000μVolts/meter, is expressed as 60 dBμV/m. This is *no longer a dimensionless number,* since x decibels above a microvolt have the dimension of a voltage.

Table 1.2 gives a simple conversion between μVolts and dBμVolts, or Volts and dB Volts.

Table 1.2—Conversion of Volts

Noise in Volts or Field in Volt/meter	Equivalent in μV or μV/meter	Corresponding dBVolts (or dBV/meter)	Corresponding dBμVolts (or dBμV/meter)
1000	10^9	60	180
316		50	170
100	10^8	40	160
32		30	150
10	10^7	20	140
3		10	130
1	10^6	0	120
.3	300,000	−10	110
.1	100,000	−20	100
.03	30,000	−30	90
.01	10,000	−40	80
.003	3,000	−50	70
.001	1,000	−60	60

1.2   Outside Sources of EMI and Their Remedies

The modern environment is crowded by *intentional* and *unintentional* radiated and conducted ambients. Knowing some measures of their typical levels is important.

1.2.1   CW Transmitters

The atmosphere is entirely saturated by electromagnetic fields generated by authorized transmitters, which operate in a range from a few tens of kHz to several 1000 MHz. Figure 1.3 gives some typical values of field levels from radio transmitters. To give an idea, one could say:

- below .01 volt/meter (10 millivolts/meter) there is no risk of EMI (unless the product itself is an RF receiver tuned in the same frequency range).

- .1 volt/meter to 3 volts/meter is the beginning of potential EMI trouble (depending upon what frequency, and the physical dimensions of the equipment. The larger they are, the higher the risk.)

- Above 3 volts/meter is a region of significant EMI risks, if no precaution is taken.

The basic protection strategy, therefore, is to reduce the field strength locally received by the equipment. This can be done by:

- using equipment casing to provide shielding,

- shielding cables coming in or out of the equipment,

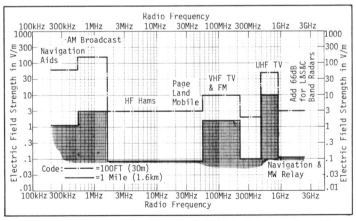

Figure 1.3—Average Values of Electromagnetic Fields in Volt/meter Caused by Radio Transmitters Located at 100 ft and 1 Mile Away.

- using internal shields around the most susceptible parts of the unit,

- modifying the physical location or orientation of the equipment,

- using aluminum paper and screen-wire to shield the entire room where the unit is installed.

If the culprit transmitter has been clearly identified, as well as the portion of the victim's circuitry which is disturbed, sometimes it is simpler to design a stop-band *(trap)* filter to eliminate a particular frequency.

1.2.2 High Frequency (Other Than Radio) Generators

Arc welders, ultrasonic machines, HF and microwave ovens are well known outside EMI sources, but there are more troublesome EMI sources, such as computers, office machines, HF switching power converters, TV games or garage-door openers. Like the previous EMI sources discussed, they create both radiated and conducted noise which couple into equipment. In addition, because of their pulsed nature, they occupy a wide frequency bandwidth which creates a potential threat to a larger number of circuits. The solutions here are basically the same as those protecting against radio transmitters, except that these sources may be closer and difficult to locate, thereby requiring greater protection, such as:

- shielding of case and cables

- physical relocation and/or reorientation

- room shielding

- filtering the power line, if this is a source of noise.

1.2.3 Broadband/Transient Sources

There is an infinity of random, non-intentional, noise sources which can surround equipment. They include:

- dimmer switches,

- burner igniters,

- dc and ac commutator motors,

- fluorescent lights, neon signs,

- automobile ignitions,

- HV overhead lines.

The basic protection principles are the same as in those shown in paragraphs 1.2.1 and 1.2.2.

1.2.4 Lightning

A lightning stroke creates a huge electromagnetic field and induces surge voltages in power and communication lines (power, telephone, video, etc.). The basic protection methods include:

- diverting energy away with lightning rods and earthing conductors,
- shielding, if lightning strokes are frequent and nearby,
- installing transient protectors on input/output lines to prevent conducted surges from reaching equipment,
- suppressing residual energy *inside* the equipment by installing secondary protection such as zener diodes or varistors (Fig. 1.4).

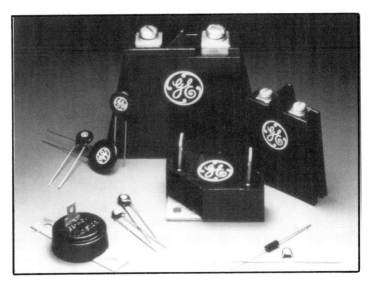

Figure 1.4—Commercial Type of Lightning Transient Protection.
(Courtesy of G.E.)

1.2.5 Electrostatic Discharge

Electrostatic discharge creates an enormous number of problems (malfunctions or permanent damages) in electronic circuitry, which are troublesome to the engineer. The basics of *what happens* are shown in Fig. 1.5 when ESD involving a human body occurs. This can also occur with any electrically charged body such as:

- plastic or fiberglass cans,
- paper,

1.7

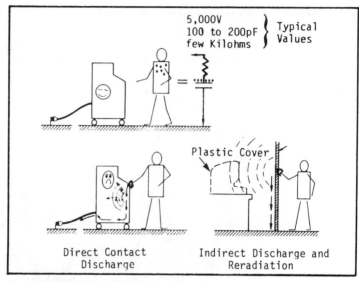

Figure 1.5—The Electrostatic Discharge Scenario.

- rubber belts,
- forced air (fans, air guns) et cetera.

Static discharges are aggravated by dry atmosphere, high personnel activity, nylon or wool carpeting, etc. Such discharges can be reduced or eliminated by:

- controlling the relative humidity
- use of anti-static spray,
- using an ionizing air-gun,
- metallic casings or conductive paints,
- bonding carefully together all metal parts and grounding them.
- shielding cables and ferrite beads on susceptible wiring.

1.2.6 Power Line Disturbances

Power line disturbances range from slow over-or-under voltage to sharp, extremely narrow transients, as shown in Fig. 1.6. The sources of such disturbances are often power-switching operations, heavy loads turning on/off, power semi-conductors operation, circuit breakers or fuses blowing, lightning induced surges, etc. A good protection scheme should consider:

- power-line filters,
- dc distribution filtering,
- packaging of filter and power components,
- shielded power cords,
- relocation of equipment on another branch circuit,
- isolation (shielded) transformers,
- checking of grounding conductors at noise source.

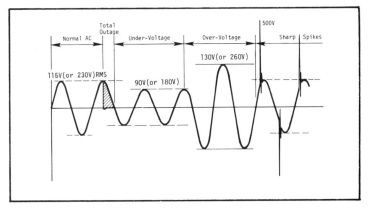

Figure 1.6—Power Line Disturbances.

Summary

- EMI problems occur because the 3 following conditions exist simultaneously:

    —noise source

    —coupling path

    —susceptible or "victim" equipment

- Acting on one or more of these conditions will affect EMI
- Modern society is replete with intentional or fortuitous sources and victims
- Coupling can exist by conduction and/or radiation.

2   PCB Design and Layout

The following chapter covers the noise generation and susceptibility aspect of electronic components and the proper PCB layout to overcome EMI problems at the first elementary building block of a device.

2.1 Components Properties Regarding Noise

For noise-free design of printed circuit boards (PCB's), parasitic behavior of integrated and discrete components must be understood. Because of elements which are seldom shown on circuits or specs, but which are physically present (such as stray capacitance, parasitic inductance, unwanted feedback), analog and digital devices will respond to stimuli to which they should not, inductances will become by-pass and capacitors will behave like chokes.

2.1.1 The Problem of Analog Circuits

Analog devices may exhibit either or both of two EMI problems: (1) undesired low-level coupling into sensitive circuits, and/or (2) non-linear, high-level coupling due to audio-rectification. Low-level coupling results from one or more of the following propagation paths:

- Common-impedance coupling resulting in voltage drop from power supply and/or return rails and/or interconnecting leads.

- Radiated fields coupling directly into the wiring containing the victim analog device.

- Crosstalk in circuits, power distribution and backplane interconnects.

Figure 2.1 illustrates common-impedance coupling between two circuits resulting from an external current, I_g, flowing in a common return path, discrete wire, wire trace or ground plane. This situation can also develop from the supply bus which is common to two or more circuits which have inadequate decoupling.

Another EMI problem can develop for conducted RF emissions above one volt of differential mode, viz., audio-recitification. Figure 2.2 shows the traditional $S = N$ passband level below cutoff in a baseband amplifier (Case #1). Here the amplifier offers no rejection to interference appear-

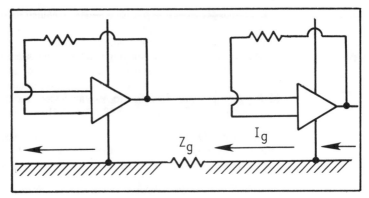

Figure 2.1—Common-Impedance Coupling in Circuits from an External Flowing Current.

ing below cutoff. Beyond cutoff, the amplifier rejects interfering emissions by an amount determined by the slope selectivity, similar to a filter response (Case #2). For the far out-of-band region $f_{EMI} >> F_{co}$ in Fig. 2.2 in amplifiers and digital logic, the figure indicates that the *ideal* response may continue indefinitely. This does not happen in reality due to *audio-rectification*. A frequency region (see star) is reached in the stop band in which anti-resonance response, from parasitic wiring capacitance and inductance, takes place as suggested in Case #3. These RF *windows* cause the out-of-band responses to be much less than the ideal rejection. In some cases, the rejection may be as little as 20 dB (or less) relative to that of the pass band.

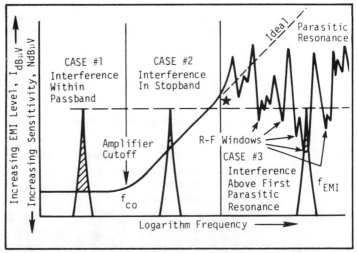

Figure 2.2—Audio-Rectification Phenomena on Amplifiers and Logic Circuits.

The audio-recitification phenomenon is explained by the fact that any active device exhibits a degree of non-linearity, especially at saturation levels. When the victim, for example, is overdriven, the RF carrier is rectified by an emitter-base junction and the carrier *sees* a low capacitance reactance to ground, such as in the second detector of a superhet receiver. The modulation envelope is recovered and processed through the rest of the amplifer. Audio-rectification explains why a radar can jam a computer, or a citizen's band (CB) can cause EMI to a stereo amplifier. It is a recurring EMI problem in all active electronic devices.

2.1.2 Some Logic Families

In terms of EMI susceptibility, digital logic is very different from analog because of both sensitivity and bandwidth considerations. Sensitivity of logic is measured by its noise-immunity voltage level, typically on the order of a few hundred millivolts. This may be contrasted with analog devices in which sensitivity may vary from nanovolts to millivolts (a few analog devices have sensitivities corresponding to a volt or higher).

Most analog devices have relatively narrow bandwidths, i.e., less than 1 MHz. In contrast to this, the bandwidth of all logic is greater than 1 MHz. The popular TTL logic has a bandwidth of about 30 MHz, for example, and the high-speed logic families have more than 100 MHz. Thus, while logic tends to be more immune to narrowband EMI than analog devices, it may be more susceptible because of its enormous bandwidth occupancy, viz., it falls within the frequency range of many sources.

Table 2.1 lists typical characteristics of various digital logic families. The bandwidth is shown as $1/\pi\tau_r$, τ_r being the rise time measured between the 0.1 to 0.9 amplitude points. Some switching-state transition currents are listed and the table shows CMOS current to be very low relative to the high-speed family. Several of the entries in Table 2.1 will be used in later illustrative examples to compute specific thresholds or immunities.

The noise-immunity level is that level above which a "0" state might flip to a "1" or vice versa. The ac noise margin is equal to or greater than the dc noise margin.

Figure 2.3 shows a parallel between the noise rejection of a TTL gate in the time domain and in the frequency domain. Although for noise glitches shorter than 10 nsec, the gate should not be activated, it will if the amplitude is sufficiently high, i.e., 1 volt for 5 nsec pulse duration. The reciprocal of this is shown in the frequency domain where the same TTL gate is pictured as a LOW PASS filter. Above a certain frequency (which is shown in the column *bandwidth* of Table 2.1), it re-

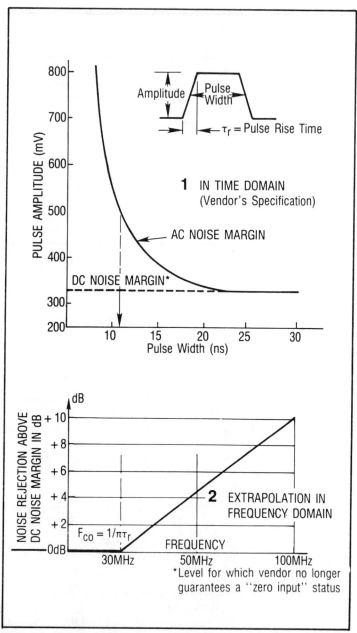

Figure 2.3—Example of a Noise Rejection of a Logic Circuit (LS-TTL), in Time (1) and Frequency (2) Domains.

Table 2.1—Typical Characteristics of Various Logic Families.

Logic Families	Output Voltage Swing	Rise/Fall Time (ns)	Bandwidth (MHz) $1/\pi\tau_r$	Power Supply Transition Current (mA)	Input C (pF)	PS Current* Per Gate Drive (mA)	DC Noise** Margin (mV)
Emitter Coupled Logic (ECL-10K)	0.8V	2/2	160	< 1	3	1.2	100
Emitter Coupled Logic (ECL-100K)	0.8V	0.75	420	< 1	3	0.5	100
Transistor-Transistor Logic (TTL)	3V	10	32	16	5	1.5	400
Low Power TTL (LP-TTL)	3V	20/10	21	8	5	1.6	400
Schottky TTL Logic (STTL)	3V	3/2.5	120	30	4	4	300
Low-Power Schottky TTL (LS-TTL)	3V	10/6	40	8	6	2.1	300
Complementary Metal Oxide Logic (CMOS) 5V or (15V)	5V (15V)	90/100 (50)	3 (6)	1 (10)	5	0.2	1V (4.5)
High Speed CMOS (5V)	5V	10	32	10	5	1	1V

*Peak instantaneous current that the driving device has to feed into each driven gate.
**DC Noise Margin = Difference between V_{OUT} of driving gate and V_{in} required by driven gate to recognize a "1" or "0".

jects the noise, but only to a certain extent. The reciprocal of this is that fast logic with wide bandwidths generates a lot of noise in the upper frequencies. Since several contributors may concur simultaneously on a PCB to upset the logic, Table 2.2 may be used as a *Budget of what not to exceed* for each contributor.

Besides their differences due to technology, the vulnerability of a logic circuit depends on:

- The circuit function. The table above is given for a typical gate. Other circuits (counters, triggers, drivers, decoders, etc.), although working with compatible levels, may exhibit different input impedances.

- What the circuit is doing when a parasitic pulse appears on its input: For instance, an inverter gate will be more susceptible to positive spike when its input is in a logical "0", and vice versa.

- What is the criticality of the stressed line? The classical example is the "RESET" line on a µP chip which, if activated by a noise glitch, will wipe-out the undergoing transaction.

- The maximum "NOT TO EXCEED" levels of the technology. Ultra short transients above 30 volts can permanently overstress FET and MOS chips. Negative transients can bring CMOS devices into a "latch-up" mode, requiring a power-off to resume to normal.

2.2   Printed Circuit Board: The First Building Block

The PCB is the first brick in the electronic package. If the first brick is not right, the building won't stand. A multitude of EMC *war stories* show that an in depth look at PCB design would have saved thousands of dollars in testing, late-fixes, re-testing. etc., of a complete equipment. Therefore, look first at the PCB layout to accomplish the noise budget of Table 2.2.

Table 2.2—*Example of Internal Noise Budget Allocation for Logic Circuits.*

Noise Source	Budget	TTL	ECL-10K
Power Supply	20%	80mV	20mV
Voltage Distribution IZ Drop	20%	80mV	20mV
Data Line Mismatch and Reflections:	20%	80mV	20mV
Cross Talk	20%	80mV	20mV
External Radiation Pickup	20%	80mV	20mV
Total Noise:	100%	400mV	100mV

2.2.1   Voltage Distribution and Zero-Volt Return

2.2.1.1   Decoupling

Power distribution on PCBs is traditionally provided by supply and return traces. Their impedance (inductive reactance) is unimportant for slow-speed and/or low-power logic such as CMOS. Capacitor decoupling is not needed except at the connector input. As the logic speed increases, for example TTL, considerably more care in layout is required due to increased common-impedance coupling. High-frequency ceramic-disc caps come to the rescue with one used to serve typically two DIP chips.

The so-called *decoupling* capacitor can be regarded as a reservoir to provide the inrush current that the logic device needs to switch in the specified time. The reason for this is that by no means can the long wiring from the power-supply regulator to the chip provide the peak current without excessive voltage drop. The value of the decoupling capacitor C, close to the logic elements (chips) requiring the switching current, I is:

$$C = \frac{I}{dV/dt} \qquad (2.1)$$

where, dV = voltage variation at capacitor output (supply rail sag) caused by the demand of a current I during the time interval, dt.

dt = logic switching time.

I = transient current demand of the logic family.

Table 2.3 lists values of C for some popular logic families based on a maximum allowable V_{cc} drop equal to 20% of Noise Immunity Level.*

Some guidelines should be followed to insure that C works properly as a decoupling capacitor. Figure 2.4 shows a layout of power supply and return traces which are too far apart and therefore a poor design

Table 2.3—Decoupling Caps for Some Popular Logic.

Logic Family	Current Requirements		dV = 20% of NIL	dt = Rise Time	Decoupling C = ΔI/(dV/dt)
	Gate Switch	Gate Drive			
CMOS	1 mA	1 mA	200 mV	50 ns	(500 pF)**
H-CMOS***	10 mA	1 mA	200 mV	10 ns	750 pF
TTL	16 mA	8 mA	80 mV	10 ns	3000 pF
STTL	30 mA	20 mA	60 mV	3 ns	2500 pF
LSTTL	8 mA	11 mA	60 mV	8 ns	2500 pF
ECL-10K	1 mA	6 mA	20 mV	2 ns	700pF

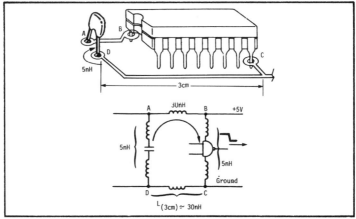

Figure 2.4—Effect of Inductance in Power Distribution.

---

*Calculation is based on only one DIP chip and one logic element driving a fanout of five gates. The noise immunity level is spread equally over five contributing noise sources: power supply, sag power distribution radiation pickup, common-impedance coupling, crosstalk and reflections due to impedance mismatch. (see Noise Budget of Table 2.2.)

**In the case of the standard (low-speed) CMOS, this value is conservative because the assumption that *the long wiring from the power supply cannot provide the peak current without excessive voltage drop* is not true. For rise times in the 50-100 ns range, even with 1μHenry of supply leads inductance, the voltage drop would be acceptable. So unless protection against severe ambient EMI is required, this decoupling is not necessary.

***Although presumably "quieter" than TTL, High Speed CMOS still exhibits a significant switching current due to its fast transition.

2.7

practice. The problem, as shown in the equivalent circuit of Fig. 2.4, results in an inductance of about 5 nH for the cap leads (assuming they are cut very short) between the 5 V and 0V traces and 5 nH for the chip and DIP pin leads. For a trace supply and return totalling 6 cm, the trace inductance is about 60 nH, so a total loop inductance of: $60 + 5 + 5 = 70$ nH.

Thus, the voltage drop from the capacitor to the IC resulting from the total loop inductance, L, is:

$$V = LdI/dt \qquad (2.2)$$

For Schottky TTL logic having a peak current demand of 30 mA/Gate, the situation of Fig. 2.4 results in a voltage drop, V:

$$V = 70 \times 10^{-9} \times (.03/3 \times 10^{-9}) = 700 \text{ mV}$$

This is much above the budget and even larger than the worst case noise immunity of this logic.

To reduce this potentially dangerous situation, Fig. 2.5 illustrates how the power supply and return traces should be routed close together, thus reducing the series inductance by about 80%, (more or less). From Eq. (2.2) then, the voltage drop would become about 100 mV, or approximately 20% of the noise-immunity level, which is acceptable.

Ultimately, the limitation of the cap high-frequency performance is predicted on the self-resonant frequency of the capacitance with its leads inductance.

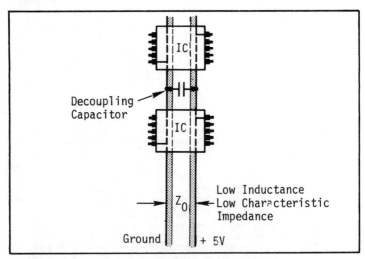

Figure 2.5—Recommended Power Rail Layout Having Low Series Inductance.

Figure 2.6 shows what are the unavoidable limitations of discrete capacitors. The critical frequency spectrum has been shown for three technologies: CMOS, TTL standard and SCHOTTKY. It can be seen that no conventional capacitor can work ideally for fast Schottky: they all behave like inductance, and may even create *ringing* instead of decoupling.

This can be reduced, however, by using either foil leads, or, better yet, the new package 2-pin DIP compatible with standard IC's for automated insertion. Such monolithic ceramic units are now available over a range from a few pF to about 10 μF. Thus, they are taking over some of the decoupling jobs formerly in the realm of tantalum units, which lose their capacitance at high frequency. Consequently, the need for the 10 μF ceramic disc cap, at the power supply PCB edge connector input will be eliminated by the use of a single monolithic ceramic, 2-pin DIP. Electronic Industries Association (EIA) (e.g., RS-198) and MIL specifications identify the basic classes of ceramic dielectrics and cap performance.

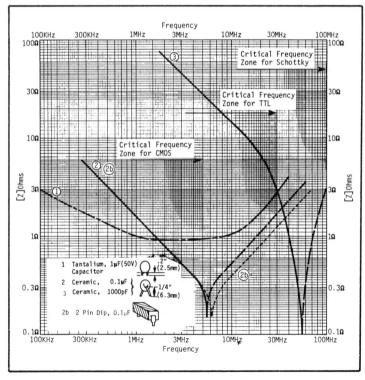

Figure 2.6—Impedance vs. Frequency of Some Typical PCB Mount Capacitors.

2.2.1.2 Other Methods of Voltage Distribution Clean-Up

Excessive reduction of voltage sag on the power distribution traces by using decoupling caps is basically *cheating*. It could be stated that the distribution system was poorly designed in the beginning. So why compound the problem by using caps (band-aid engineering), which increases expense and reduces reliability? Other solutions to the problem should be investigated:

- zero volt plane with large $+V_{dc}$ traces
- raised power bus distribution
- multi-layer boards.

Thin lines, far away from the return conductor, present a high inductance (typically 10 nanoHenrys per cm). Table 2.4 shows the impedance versus frequency of typical PCB traces.

If, for instance, two Schottky chips are *daisy-chained* on a length of 10 cm by a 1 mm supply trace, for a bandwidth of 100 MHz (which is the reciprocal $1/\pi\tau_r$ of the 3 nsec transition for Schottky), the corresponding impedance is 72.5 Ω corresponding to a voltage dip of:

$$30 \text{ mA} \times 72.5 = 2.1 \text{ volt}$$

Table 2.4—Impedance of Printed Circuits.

Freq.	w=1 mm, t=0.03 mm				w=3mm, t=0.03mm			Ohms/ Square	Freq.
	ℓ=10mm	ℓ=30mm	ℓ=100mm	ℓ=300mm	ℓ=30mm	ℓ=100mm	ℓ=300mm		
50Hz	5.74 m	17.2 m	57.4 m	172 m	5.74	19.1 m	57.4 m	813μ	50 Hz
100Hz	5.74 mΩ	17.2 mΩ	57.4 mΩ	172 mΩ	5.74 mΩ	19.1 mΩ	57.4 mΩ	813μ	100 Hz
1 kHz	5.74 mΩ	17.2 mΩ	57.4 mΩ	172 mΩ	5.74 mΩ	19.1 mΩ	57.5 mΩ	817μ	1 kHz
10 kHz	5.76 mΩ	17.3 mΩ	57.9 mΩ	174 mΩ	5.89 mΩ	20.0 mΩ	61.4 mΩ	830μ	10 kHz
100 kHz	7.21 mΩ	24.3 mΩ	92.5 mΩ	311 mΩ	14.3 mΩ	62.0 mΩ	225 mΩ	871 μ	100 kHz
300 kHz	14.3 mΩ	54.4 mΩ	224 mΩ	795 mΩ	39.9 mΩ	177 mΩ	657 mΩ	917 μ	300 kHz
1 MHz	44.0 mΩ	173 mΩ	727 mΩ	2.59 Ω	131 mΩ	590 mΩ	2.18Ω	1.01 m	1 MHz
3 MHz	131 m	516 m	2.17 Ω	7.76 Ω	395 m	1.76 Ω	6.54 Ω	1.17 m	3 MHz
10 MHz	437 mΩ	1.72 Ω	7.25 Ω	25.8 Ω	1.31 Ω	5.89 Ω	21.8 Ω	1.53 m	10 MHz
30 MHz	1.31 Ω	5.16 Ω	21.7 Ω	77.6 Ω	3.95 Ω	17.6 Ω	65.4 Ω	2.20 m	30 MHz
100 MHz	4.37Ω	17.2Ω	72.5Ω	258 Ω	13.1 Ω	58.9 Ω	218 Ω	3.72 m	100 MHz
300 MHz	13.1 Ω	51.6 Ω	217 Ω		39.5 Ω	176 Ω		6.39 m	300 MHz
1 GHz	43.7 Ω	172 Ω			131Ω			11.6 m	1 GHz

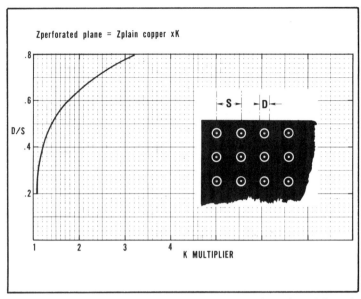

Figure 2.8—K Multiplier to Compute Impedance Increase of a Perforated Ground Plane vs. Plain Foil.

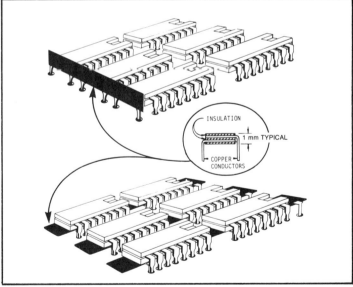

Figure 2.9—Minibus Power Distribution When a Ground Plane is Not Achievable (Rogers/Mektron).

Table 2.5—Characteristic Impedance of Different Flat Conductors Arrangements.

W/h or D/W	#1 Parallel Strips[1]	#2 Strip Over Gnd Plane[1]	#3 Strips Side by Side[2]
0.5	377	377	NA
0.6	281	281	NA
0.7	241	241	NA
0.8	211	211	NA
0.9	187	187	NA
1.0	169	169	0
1.1	153	153	25
1.2	140	140	34
1.5	112	112	53
1.7	99	99	62
2.0	84	84	73
2.5	67	67	87
3.0	56	56	98
3.5	48	48	107
4.0	42	42	114
5.0	34	34	127
6.0	28	28	137
7.0	24	24	146
8.0	21	21	153
9.0	19	19	160
10.0	17	17	166
12.0	14	14	176
15.0	11.2	11.2	188
20.0	8.4	8.4	204
25.0	6.7	6.7	217
30.0	5.6	5.6	227
40.0	4.2	4.2	243
50.0	3.4	3.4	255
100.0	1.7	1.7	293

Notes: 1. Mylar dielectric assumed; $\epsilon_r = 5.0$
       2. Paper base phenolic or glass epoxy
           assumed; $\epsilon_r = 4.7$

$$Z_{01} = (377/\sqrt{\epsilon_r})\ (h/W),\ \text{for W>3h and h>3t}$$
$$Z_{02} = (377/\sqrt{\epsilon_r})\ (h/W),\ \text{for W>3h}$$
$$Z_{03} = (120/\sqrt{\epsilon_r})\ \ell n_e\ (D/W + \sqrt{(D/W)^2 - 1}),\ \text{for W>>t}$$
$$D >> \text{nearby ground plane}$$

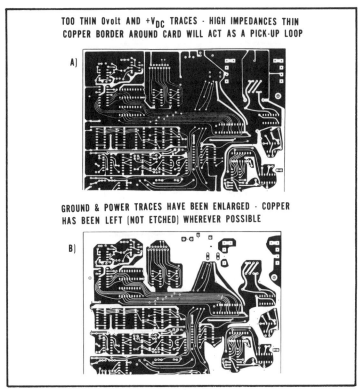

TOO THIN Ovolt AND +V$_{DC}$ TRACES - HIGH IMPEDANCES THIN COPPER BORDER AROUND CARD WILL ACT AS A PICK-UP LOOP

A)

GROUND & POWER TRACES HAVE BEEN ENLARGED - COPPER HAS BEEN LEFT (NOT ETCHED) WHEREVER POSSIBLE

B)

Figure 2.7—Enlarging Ground Areas in PCBs.

Figure 2.7A—PCB Ground Plane/Shield Retrofit. Insulated copper foil is connected to 0V traces as much as possible for shielding and 0V return improvement. Insulated double sided sandwich is used for power busing and shielding (one side). + V$_{cc}$ and 0V tabs at each DIP position.

When changing from thin or very long traces, to copper plane as in Fig. 2.7, the immediate benefit is this: a quasi-infinite plane has no external inductance—it has only resistance and internal inductance, which increase like $\sqrt{F}$ above skin depth region, instead of increasing with frequency as in the case of thin wires. For example, at the 100 MHz frequency of the previous example, a wide plane shows only 3.7 mΩ, i.e., the switching of 30 mA will cause only 100 μV drop in the common ground.

Therefore, by *leaving* the copper as much as possible rather than etching, a low-impedance common return is achieved for both the supply decreased since they are close to their return. *This preferred practice can be expressed by this guideline: Make the PCB as optically opaque as possible by extending supply and ground return traces to large areas.*

When copper planes have numerous holes in a grid pattern, impedance is increased by a factor shown in Fig. 2.8. When low-impedance planes cannot be achieved, use flat buses for power distribution (see Fig. 2.9). Thet are better against EMI than solid wires, and they also decrease the number of discrete decoupling capacitors. What flat buses provide (since they have a small L and large C) is a lower impedance. Table 2.5 shows the characteristic impedance of three different transmission lines as a function of their geometry. Thus, power distribution for serving logic will now be pictured as distributed over a transmission line. Three different potential options are shown in Table 2.5. Option #3 corresponds to side-by-side traces on the same side of the board. Option #3 would require D/W ratios of less than about 1.01 ($Z_o < 8\Omega$) which is totally impractical, unless a discrete capacitor is added as in Fig. 2.5.

Because of the large amount of area taken by copper plane, option #2 shown in Table 2.5 generally requires a multi-layer board which is discussed later. Thus, option #1 shown in the table is occasionally used for single layer, double-cladded PCB's. Physical realization of the first option is suggested in Fig. 2.9 for both horizontal and the more common vertical configuration.

For instance, option #1 from Table 2.5 shows, for a bus width of 8 mm and a spacing of .2 mm, a 4Ω characteristic impedance. The maximum voltage drop for 1 Schottky gate would then be 30 mA $\times$ 4Ω = 120 mV which is tolerable.

Finally, in extreme cases where a ground plane is needed but the wiring density does not permit it, AND a multilayer is not feasible either, Fig. 2.7a shows a *fix* option.

2.2.2 Analog/Digital Mix

When analog and digital devices are mounted on the same PCB, common-impedance coupling must be avoided (see Paragraph 2.1), because the 0V return is polluted by fast current transitions. To reduce

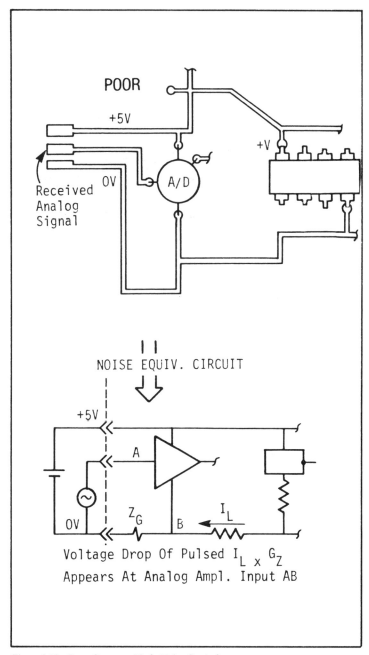

Figure 2.10—Poor Common-Mode Noise Control.

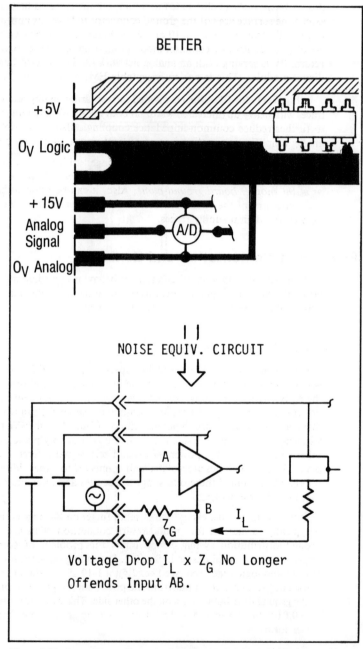

Figure 2.11—Improvement Upon the Common-Mode Noise Problem of Fig. 2.10.

this problem, one can eliminate the common-impedance path(s) and/or extend the surface area of the ground conductor to lower its impedance. Each is illustrated in Figs. 2.10 and 2.11. Figure 2.10 shows an example of poor control of common-mode ground noise. The zero voltage return, 0V is serving both an analog network (A/D converter) and the digital modules. This is not an acceptable EMI control practice.

In Fig. 2.11, the 0V return is divided into separate analog and digital traces with heavy up (increased width) in both the supply and return paths to further reduce common-impedance coupling. Also, if possible, the analog amplifier is supplied from a distinct power supply output.

The 0V return of the analog circuit no longer utilizes the noisy logic ground. *They are only commoned at the power supply 0 volt terminal, or at the mother board ground-plane.* Also, it can be noticed that the input circuitry of the A/D converter is *no more enclosed in the noisy loop* of the digital supply traces.

2.3   Physical Implementation and Zoning

With the understanding of component behavior regarding noise and power distribution requirements, this section discusses general layout of wire-wrapped, single-layer and multi-layer boards.

2.3.1   Wirewrap, Single Layer Board

For medium (e.g., TTL) and low-speed (e.g., CMOS) logic, the wirewrap board is still popular for one or a few-of-a-kind designs, or the early engineering design of the logic *breadboard.* Its convenience, no artwork or tooling, and fast turn around are some of the advantages that make wirewrap boards a popular choice. Figure 2.12 shows a typical wirewrap board with one side acting as a power supply plane and the other side acting as the power return and zero-signal reference return plane. Several pin holes are isolated and connected to either side so that pins can be mounted thereto to support discretes and interconnect wiring, i.e., the wirewrap.

In wirewrap boards, every fifth or tenth finger on the edge connector is typically earmarked for ground return connection. This provides a ground distribution system which limits the problem of common-impedance coupling discussed in Sec. 2.2. Depending upon the total load current and logic type used (see Sec. 2.1), a 1-10 μf tantalum capacitor is used at the connector input from the power supply plane on one side to the ground distribution lines on the other side. This capacitor is bridged by a 0.01-0.1 μf ceramic-disc, high frequency cap at the same connector finger location.

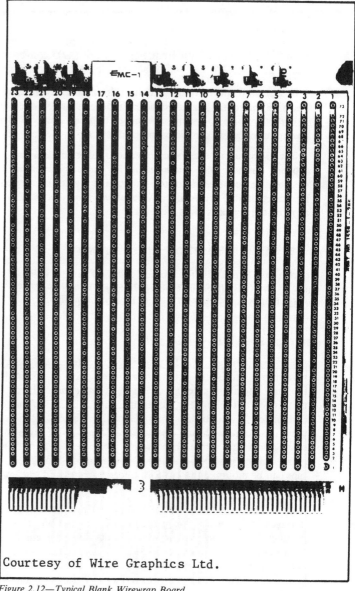

Courtesy of Wire Graphics Ltd.

Figure 2.12—Typical Blank Wirewrap Board.

The discretes (resistors, diodes, caps, etc.) and ICs are mounted first to the wirewrap board pins. A ceramic disc, high frequency cap of 1000 pf or other value (see Sec. 2.2.1) is traditionally used for every one or two DIP packages to provide decoupling. Then the Z1 wires are next mounted. In wire-wrap parlance, Z1 wires are the longer runs and are defined as all wires greater in length than D/2, where D is the diagonal dimension of the wirewrap board. These wires are routed close to the ground plane. This helps control the characteristic impedance of interconnects by reducing the self inductance of the wire. Since the longer runs, Z1, have the largest inductance, they are wired in first.

Next an option exists to reduce radiation, radiation pickup or crosstalk, by laying down an X-Y grid over the Z1 wires as shown in Fig. 2.13. This grid matrix shield also helps control characteristic impedance of Z1 and return (the grid) wires, but could be excessive for EMI control for most applications.

Following either the Z1 interconnects or the above X-Y grid, if used, the shorter Z2 wires (Z2 < D/2) are laid out. Another option exists for an X-Y grid to cover all wires for the same reasons indicated above. The routing of Z1 and Z2 wires should be laid out for the shortest path and not in an X-Y directional manner which would otherwise increase crosstalk. Thus, random crossover of wirewrap wires is best for EMI control. A completed wirewrap board might then look like that shown in Fig. 2.14.

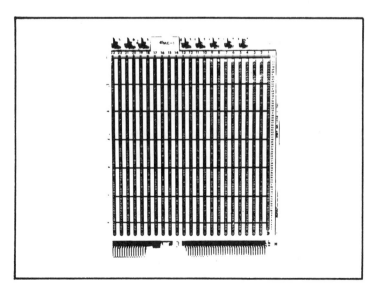

Figure 2.13—Controlling Radiation, Radiation Pickup and Interconnect Impedance with a Topside X-Y Ground Grid Configuration.

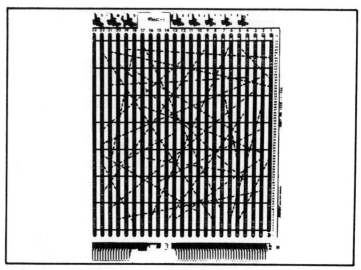

Figure 2.14—Typical Completed Wirewrap Board.

2.3.2 Single Layer PC Boards

Printed circuit boards are generally laid out whereby the higher-speed devices (fast logic, clock oscillators, etc.) are located closer to the edge connector and the lower-speed logic and memory, if applicable, are located furthest from the connector as shown in Fig. 2.15. This tends to compound common-impedance coupling, radiation and crosstalk. Of course, the same could also apply to wirewrap boards discussed in Chapter 3.

If the highest logic speed is below TTL, then layout is relatively unimportant from an EMI point of view. The single exception is for *optical isolators, isolations transformers or filters which should be located as close to the edge connector as possible.*

Regarding power distribution, the consequence of too much separation between power supply and return rails was discussed in paragraph 2.2.2. This is now illustrated in Fig. 2.16 in which a poor PCB layout scheme is used whereby the supply trace appears across the top and the return trace progresses across the bottom of the board. This results in undesired high self-inductance, greater circuit crosstalk, and excessive trace radiation.

To preclude the problem depicted in Fig. 2.16, the PCB layout scheme shown in Fig. 2.17 should be used. Here, the power supply and return

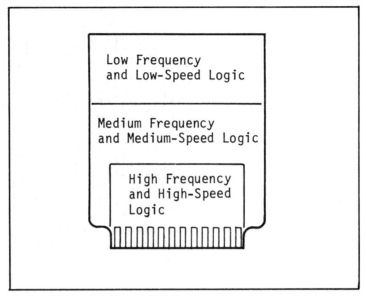

Figure 2.15—Functional Layout Guidelines.

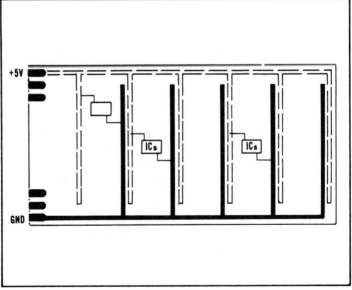

Figure 2.16—A Bad Layout Giving High Inductance and Few Adjacent Signal Return Paths, Which Leads to Crosstalk.

traces are located close together on the PCB to form a transmission line which significantly reduces the distribution impedance. Vertical extension of the transmission line concept is possible via feeder traces on the top side of the board at the left and right connected by plated thru-holes. The layout in Fig. 2.17 also helps (1) in reducing circuit crosstalk, since fields are confined to a tighter configuration and (2) reduces overall radiation from the board since signal trace returns have lesser loop areas. Figure 2.18 is a further extension of the EMC benefits over the layout in Fig. 2.17.

Similar to wire wrap boards, about every tenth pin on the edge finger connector of PCB's is typically planned for ground return as shown in Fig. 2.18. The regulated power bus at the edge connector is decoupled by a 1-10 μf tantalum capacitor, depending upon the total load current. This capacitor is shunted by a 0.01-0.1 μf high-frequency, ceramic disc capacitor.

For the high-speed logic family, interconnect leads formed by microstrip traces above a ground plane constitute an impedance discontinuity at any abrupt change in direction, such as a 90° corner. To reduce the VSWR of this capacitance discontinuity, the right-angle corners are 45° truncated as shown in the insert Fig. 2.19. This practice is not necessary for TTL logic or lower-speed logic.

The problem with microstrip is that power traces take up both sides of a printed circuit board. Trace crossovers are virtually impossible, but

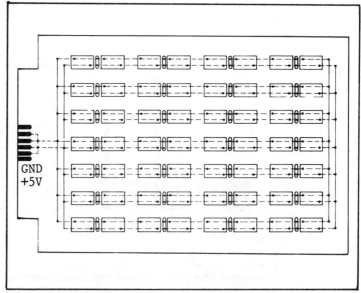

Figure 2.17—Better Layout than Fig. 2.16 to Reduce Power Distribution and Logic-Return Impedances, Trace Crosstalk and Board Radiation.

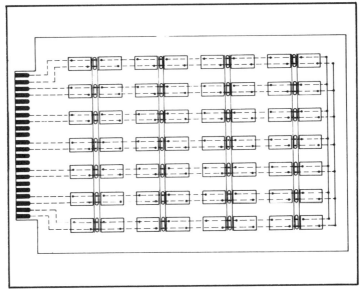

Figure 2.18—Better Layout than Fig. 2.17 for Further EMI Problem Reductions.

can be easily eliminated provided power is distributed via elevated buses as described in Sec. 2.2.1. If elevated bus-power distribution is not possible or wanted, then multi-layer boards may be the only remaining option.

Connectors must be treated as follows:

- Power-supply decoupling capacitors (serving the whole card) and I/O lines filtering capacitors (for the lines which have not been cleaned-up at the box interface) must be located very close to the edge fingers, using short and large traces.

- *Signal Isolations Transformers and Optical Isolators* must be mounted close to their input lines, and avoiding parasitic coupling with their output lines.

2.3.3 The Ultimate Answer to PCB Noise Suppression— Multilayer Boards

Generally, it is difficult to successfully operate high-speed logic on a single-layer board because of common-impedance coupling. While articles exist in trade journals describing the success of such single-layer board achievements, they require considerably more attention to pertinent fabrication details. This often makes quality control and repeatability difficult during mass production. In an attempt to avoid such problems,

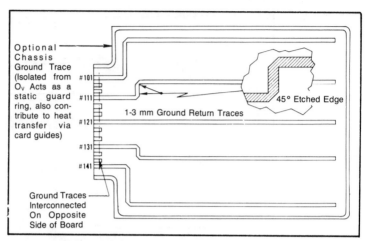

Figure 2.19—PCB Logic Ground Return Layout.

including excessive radiation and pickup, multi-layer boards are recommended wherein the power supply and return, and zero-signal reference are all realized typically on separate one-ounce, copper foil planes.

A multilayer board is defined as two or more PCB's sandwiched together and the levels interconnected through plated thru-holes. There are usually n + 1 levels for an n-layer board as suggested in Figs. 2.20 and 2.21. Here a five-level, four-layer board configuration is illustrated. Level A is the component side and includes the interconnect traces. Together with the upper face of level B, they form a microstrip line. The upper and lower faces of ground return level B are electrically isolated by about 50 dB.* Thus, currents flowing on the lower face of level B are not seen on the upper face and vice versa.

Level C contains more interconnect lines and are usually routed perpendicular to those of level A. This permits crossover on level A to be made on level C and vice versa. The lower face of planar level B forms microstrip lines with the interconnects of level C. In a like manner the interconnects of level D form microstrip lines with the planar level E. To avoid crosstalk, interconnect traces on levels C and D are routed perpendicularly.

Levels E and B form the power supply and return planes to facilitate low-impedance distribution. Depending upon their spacing and dielectric constant, they provide a distributed board capacitance of the order of 10-1000 pF/cm^2. Since the lower face of level E is also electrically isolated from its upper face, the plane of level E also serves as a shield to contain off-the-board radiation or pickup. Should remaining radiation or pickup from the traces of level A prove to be excessive, then level A can be topped with a plane similar to level E.

---

*The skin depth of copper at 100 MHz is about 0.2 mil ≈ 5 μm. Since one-ounce foil is about five skin depths at 100 MHz, the attenuation across the thickness is 8.7 dB × 6 ≈ 52 dB.

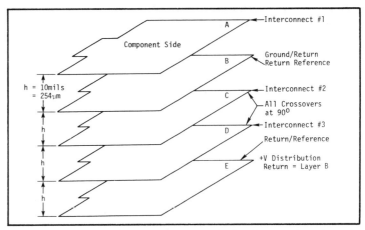

Figure 2.20—Digital Multi-Layer Board for High-Speed Logic Impedance Control.

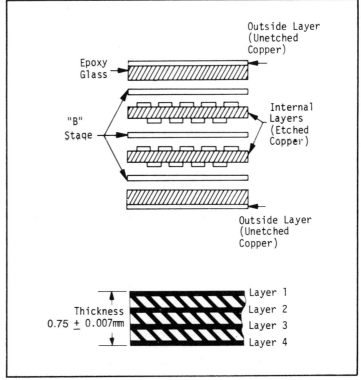

Figure 2.21—One Example of a Multilayer Board.

A variation of multi-layer boards is Multi-Pac,* which is an assembly of stacked PCB's held together in a *sandwich* with press-fit contacts, as shown in Fig. 2.22. Some principal differences between multi-layer and Multi-Pac features are:

- Multi-Pac has via or pass-thru holes from plane-to-plane, whereas with multi-layer, holes must be drilled through all circuit layers prohibiting circuitry in that area. Multi-Pac offers up to eight levels of circuitry, or solid copper sheets can be used in place of PC boards for high-current capacity.

- Controlled impedance with uniform board spacing is especially important for high-speed logic circuits.

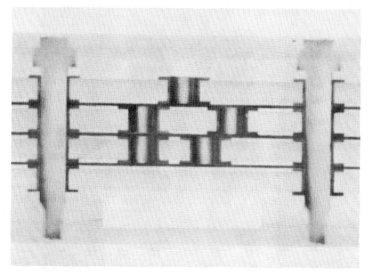

Figure 2.22—Edge Elevation View of Multi-Pac Board. (Courtesy of Multi-Pac Corp.)

- Multi-Pac permits hybrid systems into any or all parts of the board. Unlike multi-layer, Multi-Pac will allow additional circuit layers to be stacked on sections of the backpanel or daughter board where additional density is needed.

- Because Multi-Pac is a stack of discrete PC boards, any board can be changed up to assembly time when the contacts are pressed in place.

- Repairability—Contacts can be removed with Multi-Pac, and circuit layers can actually be accessed for changes or repairs.

- Moisture-in-moisture-out. Multi-Pac meets MIL-STD-202, method 103, test B for humidity; and 101 test B for salt spray.

---

*Off the shelf press-fit stacked board are also available from:
—HADCO, 12 B Manor Parkway, Salem, NH 03079 (USA)
—ELFAB, 15 Sutton's Park, London Road, Earley, Reading, RG5 1A2 (UK)

2.3.4 Multi-Wire Boards

A multi-wire circuit board, while resembling a PCB, is a customized pattern of insulated #34 AWG wires laid down on an adhesive-coated substrate by a high-speed, numerically-controlled machine as shown in Fig. 2.23. The polymide insulation, rated at 2,000 volt breakdown, makes it possible to cross the wires as close as 0.07 mm clearance without shorting out. Since cross-over capacitance is less than 1 pf, crosstalk is negligible. Figure 2.24 illustrates the general fabrication approach which permits high density packaging applications. Thus, circuits which would require many levels of wire wrapping or several layers of PCB can be reduced to a single board of 1 mm thickness, more or less.

Figure 2.23—Multiwire Machine Head Laying Down Insulated Wires in an Adhesive Substrate.

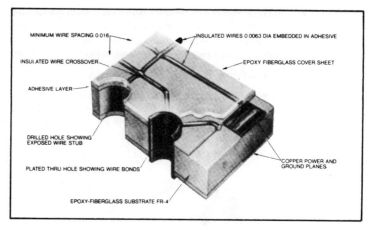

Figure 2.24—Expanded View of Typical Multiwire Board Realizability.

Uniform wire width and spacing reduces variations in applications requiring multiple supply voltages and ground planes, for controlled characteristics impedance (e.g., high-speed logic).

Its nominal 55-ohm characteristic impedance, however, requires the traditional use of high-frequency decoupling caps, mostly eliminated on multi-layer PCB's. Such carefully-controlled impedances, however, are ideal for high-speed logic interconnects to control backporching and other waveform problems.

From the designer's and fabricator's point-of-view, the multi-wire process differs significantly from the traditional steps involved ranging from circuit concept to completed board. Any fabrication process utilizing the multi-wire technique must be accomplished by or through the Multi-Wire Division* which owns the design and manufacturing rights of the product. A customer may be licensed to design and manufacture such products, but he must provide the following information:

- Board overall configuration and fabrication data,
- Ground and voltage-distribution definition with edge connection finger locations and dimensions,
- Component locations and designations,
- A net list of *from/to* list.

2.3.5 Reciprocity Between Susceptibility and Emission

What has been said up to now to make the PCB immune to self-jamming and ambient EMI is totally reciprocal, viz., radiation. A well designed PCB, with minimum loop sizes, all signal traces running close

---

*Multi-Wire Division, Kollmorgen Corporation, 31 Sea Cliff Ave., Glen Cove, New York 11542.

to their returns or, better, above their return plane, will not radiate excessive levels, and therefore, will not cause the equipment to exceed FCC, VDE or MIL-461 radiated emission limits. In addition to this, some precautions can help reduce emissions:

- select a slower (CMOS) or quieter (ECL) logic whenever possible.

- use low profile chip sockets, or use direct chip soldering. Figure 2.26 shows that the radiating loop area for 1 chip can easily reach .4 cm^2, i.e., 25 chips represent a 10 cm^2 radiating area!

- watch for long signal traces which run all around the card. On Fig. 2.25, for instance, the run FGHIJDE is a potential radiating area.

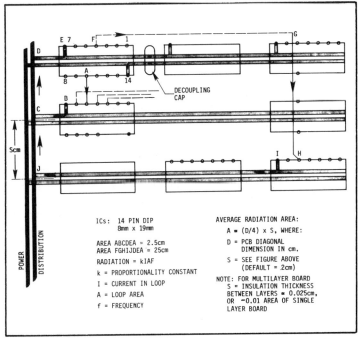

Figure 2.25—Radiation Loop Areas from Double-Sided, Single-Layer Board.

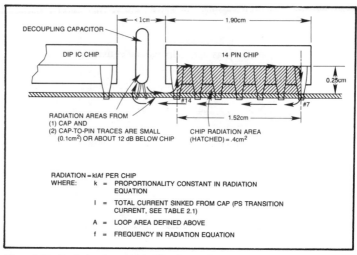

Figure 2.26—Radiation from 14-Pin Chip, During Gate Switching, Due to Instantaneous Supply Current Only. (For this aspect, flat packs or lead-less packages exhibit less radiation).

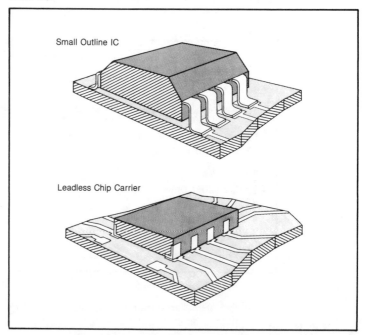

Figure 2.27—The Use of Surface Mount Components (SMC) Provides a Minimum of 2 to 1 Reduction in the Chip-to-Traces Area. This lessens both radiated emission and susceptibility problems and decreases parasitic inductance as well (see Sec. 2.2.1).

Summary

- A successful EMI design starts at board level.

**Wire-Wrapped and Single-Layer PC Board Layout
(One or Two Sided)**

- Allocate about 10% spaced connector pins to PCB ground lines.
- Route dedicated ground lines and $V_{DC} \geq 1$ mm wide.
- Dedicate ground lines for high-gain analog circuits.
- Landfill open areas with ground plane (or do not etch away: when viewed by transparency, board should look as opaque as possible).
- Check for crosstalk on long / / signal runs: if crosstalk budget (20 mV MAX. for ECL, 0.1V for TTL and Schottky, 0.2 V CMOS) is exceeded, increase wire spacing, or add a grounded guard trace between.
- Implement necessary changes in computer aided design or design automation ground rules.
- Decouple V_{DC} at connector with
  1 μF tantalum capacitor
  .01μF H-F ceramic disk or monolithic capacitor
  (.001 μF for high-speed logic).
- Decouple V_{DC} for every 2 DIP with
  .01 μF H-F ceramic disk capacitor (.001 μF for high-speed logic).
- Consider option: raised power distribution for high-speed logic.

Multilayer Boards

- Multilayers, at extra cost, provide an excellent noise reduction which might eliminate the need for extensive box shielding.
- Prefer the arrangement with voltage and ground planes *outside* and signal layers *inside.*
- When signal traces are adjacent, check for crosstalk (as in single layer PCB).

3 Motherboard Design and Layout

After a correct PCB design has been established, the next step is to proceed with the backplane or motherboard design. The same techniques used in wirewrap and PCB's are used in backplanes.

- A *Backplane* is a printed circuit (or wire-wrapped board) performing *interconnections* between the plugged-in PCB.

- A *Motherboard* is a large printed circuit on which smaller PCB's (daughters) are plugged and which also has components (bulky discrete components, power supplies, etc.).

- A *Planar Board* is a large unique board which contains a composite of integrated circuits, discrete and electromechanical devices and the I/O connectors.

One problem with motherboards is that dimensions are larger and therefore all noise mechanisms are aggravated by one order of magnitude. For instance:

- Since long parallel runs *(highways)* exist from one card location to another, they create *crosstalk* (which is seldom a problem with smaller PCB's).

- Lines become *electrically long* and may require impedance matching, etc.

Because backplanes may be carrying hundreds of interconnect lines, which are in a switching state during any given strobe gate, the propensity for radiation is severe. One traditional way to suppress this in terms of wirewrap backplanes is to lay down a grounded X-Y grid matrix on top of the wirewrap backplane, as shown in Fig. 3.1. A better method, which also improves quality control and lowers cost, is to replace the wire-wrap backplane with a PCB backplane. This method usually leads to multi-layer backplanes for the same reason that multi-layer PCB's are used over the dual-sided, single-layer boards.

A good way to start *at the first place, before all PCB layouts are frozen,* is to do the connector pin assignment and trace routes at the *motherboard.* By doing this, *forbidden* or *dangerous* vicinities can be avoided.

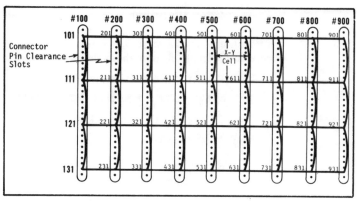

Figure 3.1—X-Y Ground-Grid Matrix in Backplane Wiring.

For instance, organize the runs by families so that:

- No high-speed clock traces run close to sensitive traces (analog, alarm, reset) or to wire going to I/O connectors (interfacing outside world).

- No high speed clocks or data wires should run without the protection of 0 volt trace next to them.

- About every 10 connector pins is a 0 volt pin.

- The + Vdc distribution runs close to the 0V traces or *plane*.

3.1 Crosstalk Between Traces

Crosstalk occurs when a wire carrying fast signals is running close to another wire. The *culprit* wire induces, by mutual capacitance and inductance, a certain percent of its voltage into the *victim* wire. Crosstalk increases when:

- culprit and victim wires run close to each other.

- the frequency of culprit signal increases (or the rise time is faster).

- the victim has a high impedance.

- culprit and victim are far from the 0 volt return.

Crosstalk is expressed in dB by the formula:

$$\text{Xtalk}_{dB} = 20 \ \text{Log}_{10} \ (\text{V induced in victim/V culprit})$$

So −20 dB of crosstalk means for 1 volt of culprit voltage, .1 volt peak will appear on the victim.

Table 3.1 gives average values of capacitive crosstalk (the one which predominates because of the high dielectric constant of epoxy) for 1 cm of trace length. For longer runs, the crosstalk increases accordingly. The procedure to apply in using the table is the following:

- Select the geometry corresponding to the culprit-victim cross section.
- Define culprit critical frequency or rise time.
- Find the corresponding crosstalk per unit length (cm).
- Apply length correction $= 20 \; \text{Log}_{10} \; \ell_{cm}$ (do not use above $\ell \geq \frac{1}{4}$ culprit wavelength).
- Apply impedance correction if $Z_{victim} \neq 100 \; \Omega$ by computing

$$20 \; \text{Log}_{10} \; \frac{Z_{victim}}{100 \; \Omega}$$

Example: two traces have a 10 cm parallel trip.

Trace width $W = 20$ mils (0.5 mm)
Trace separation $S = 20$ mils (0.5 mm)
No ground plane
Culprit = Schottky Logic, 4 volts swing, 3 nanosec rise time
Victim = Schottky Logic, Noise margin typical 1 volt, wst case 0.4 volts (input *low*)
Victim impedances = one gate *low* output impedance (about 50 Ω) on driving side, parallel with one gate *low* input impedance (about 1000Ω) on load side so total victim impedance = 46 Ω
Xtalk = -38 dB (table value) $+ 20 \; \text{Log}_{cm}$ (length correction) $+ 20 \; \text{Log} \; 46/100$ (impedance correction)
Xtalk = -38 dB $+ 20$ dB $+ (-7$ dB$) = -25$ dB $\approx 5\%$
$V_{victim} = 4$ volts $\times .05 = 200$mV

This is about one half of the *worst case* signal line noise margin, so normally no problem can be expected. However, if several adjacent culprit lines, or fan-out of several devices are running close to the victim trace, capacitive crosstalk may build up enough to upset the threshold of the receiving gate.

Table 3.1—Capacitive Crosstalk Between PCB Traces for Zvictim ≈ 100Ω.

FREQ. / W/S (Ccv, pF/cm)	W/h = 10 (Cvg = 3.5pF/cm) .3 (.10)	1 (.20)	3 (.27)	W/h = 3 (Cvg = 1pF/cm) .3 (.10)	1 (.20)	3 (.27)	W/h = 1 (Cvg = .35pF/cm) .3 (.10)	1 (.20)	3 (.27)	W/h = .3 or no gnd return below traces .3 (.10)	1 (.20)	3 (.27)	Culprit Pulse Rise Time
1kHz	-144	-138	-136	-144	-136	-136	-144	-138	-136	-144	-138	-136	
3kHz	-134	-128	-126	-134	-128	-126	-134	-128	-126	-134	-128	-126	
10kHz	-124	-118	-116	-124	-118	-116	-124	-118	-116	-124	-118	-116	
30kHz	-114	-108	-106	-114	-108	-106	-114	-108	-106	-114	-108	-106	10µs
100kHz	-104	-98	-96	-104	-98	-96	-104	-98	-96	-104	-98	-96	3µs
300kHz	-94	-88	-86	-94	-88	-86	-94	-88	-86	-94	-88	-86	1µs
1MHz	-84	-78	-76	-84	-78	-76	-84	-78	-76	-84	-78	-76	300ns
3MHz	-74	-68	-66	-74	-68	-66	-74	-68	-66	-74	-68	-66	100ns
10MHz	-64	-58	-56	-64	-58	-56	-64	-58	-56	-64	-58	-56	30ns
30MHz	-55	-49	-47	-54	-48	-46	-54	-48	-46	-54	-48	-46	10ns
100MHz	-46	-40	-38	-44	-38	-36	-44	-38	-36	-44	-38	-36	3ns
300MHz	-39	-33	-31	-36	-30	-28	-35	-30	-28	-34	-30	-28	1ns
1GHz	-34	-28	-26	-28	-22	-20	-26	-20	-18	-24	-18	-16	.3ns
3GHz	-32	-26	-24	-23	-17	-16	-15	-12	-11	-14	-8	-6	.1ns
10GHz	-31	-25	-23	-21	-15	-14	-13	-10	-8	-4	0	0	.03ns

NOTES:
- Epoxy glass assumed ($\varepsilon_r = 4$)
- Xtalk given as $20\,Log_{10}\,Vvictim/Vculprit$ per cm of parallel run. For other lengths, add $20\,Log_{10}\,\ell$ cm
- For Z victim $\neq 100\Omega$ (10 to 300Ω), add $20\,Log_{10} Zvictim/100$
- • Clamp to 0dB, Xtalk cannot be positive
- Example of some typical values = W = 20mils (.5mm) S = 30mils (.75 mm) for single layer, h = 30-40mils (.7 to 1mm). For multilayer h = 5mils (.12mm)

$$Xtalk_{dB} = 20\,Log_{10}\frac{Z_v}{Z_v + \dfrac{1}{jC_{cv}\omega}} = 20\,Log_{10}\frac{RC_{cv}\omega}{R\omega(C_{cv}+C_{vg})+1}$$

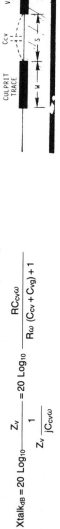
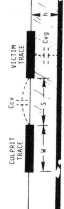

3.2   Impedance Matching

With the longer dimensions of mother boards, termination of interconnect lines which are longer than twice the one-way delay is essential
to avoid pulse ringing with high-speed logic. Correctly terminated lines
will:

- Reduce line noise by eliminating reflections.

- Reduce crosstalk.

- Avoid pulse backporching when two-way delay, 2T, of line exceeds
  rise time, T_r, of signal.

C = velocity of propagation in free space = 3×10^8 m/sec

$= 30/\sqrt{\varepsilon_r}$ cm/nsec in a dielectric line having a relative dielectric
constant ε_r

$= 20$ cm/nsec in lines with dielectric constants, $\varepsilon_t \sim 2$

$T = \ell\sqrt{\varepsilon_r}/30 \simeq 0.05\ell$; line length, ℓ, in cm

When T exceeds $T_r/2$, or when:

ℓ cm $\geqslant 10\ T_r$ (for a fan-out = 1), and
ℓ cm $\geqslant 10\ T_r/\sqrt{N}$ (for fan-out $N > 1$),

it becomes imperative to terminate the line in a resistance equal to the
line characteristic impedance; Figure 3.2 shows the problem of line matching. The decision of line matching versus rise time can be made by using
the graph in Fig. 3.3 or Table 3.2, which has been computed for ECL.

3.3   Connector Areas at Motherboard Interface

The I/O connectors area must continue the PCB-motherboard noise-
free concept. Preferably, if high speed rates are concerned, the connectors areas must respect the impedance matching, like the PC traces and
the cables, which means that alternate signal-zero volt pins may have
to be provided at the connector to avoid discontinuities in characteristic
impedance (see Fig. 3.5). In any case, an extension of the board zero
volt traces or plane underneath the connector area is recommended (Fig.
3.5). It allows a most direct connection of all the I/O signals ground
returns, and makes it easier to achieve a direct coupling of noisy lines
at connector level by discrete or *array* capacitors (also see Sec. 6: Final
Box Design).

Table 3.2—Maximum Unterminated Line Lengths vs. Characteristic Impedance and Fanout (Computed for ECL-10K to Maintain Reflection Less Than 35% Overshoot, 12% Undershoot).

Characteristics Impedance Z_0 in Ohms	Maximum Line Length in Centimeters			
	Fanout = 1	Fanout = 2	Fanout = 4	Fanout = 8
MICROSTRIP: Propagation Delay 0.148 ns/in (58 picosec/cm)				
50	21.1	19.1	17.0	14.5
68	17.8	15.7	12.7	10.2
75	17.5	15.0	11.7	9.1
90	16.5	13.7	9.9	7.6
100	16.3	13.0	9.1	6.6
BACKPLANE: Propagation Delay 0.14 ns/in (55 picosec/cm)				
100	16.8	13.7	9.7	7.1
140	15.0	10.9	7.1	4.8
180	13.2	9.1	5.3	3.3

(From MOTOROLA ECL Application Note)

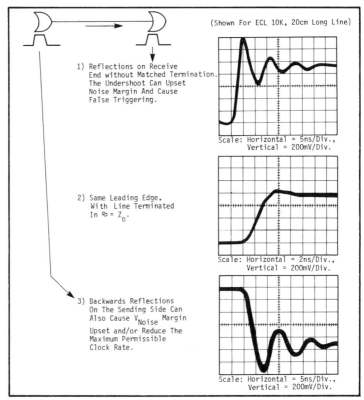

Figure 3.2—Examples of Termination Problems with Fast Logic.

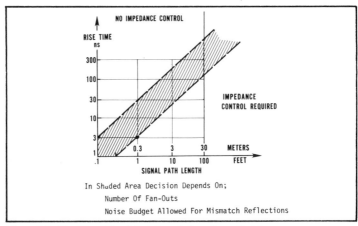

Figure 3.3—Rise Time/Signal Path Length Impedance Decision.

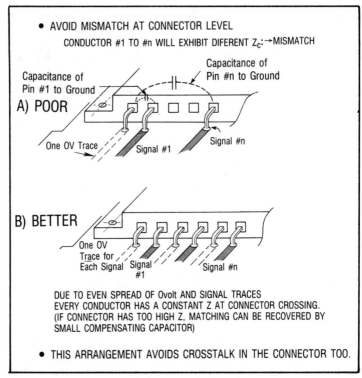

Figure 3.4—Interconnections of PC Board to Motherboard or I/O Cable for High-Speed Circuits.

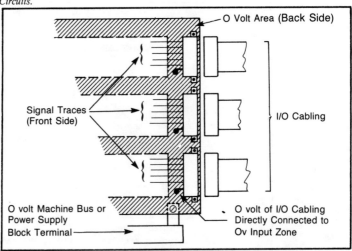

Figure 3.5—Treatment of Motherboards and Planar Boards I/O Interface.

Summary

- First do the pin assignment of the motherboard connectors.

- Avoid close parallel runs of high frequency clocks and signals with sensitive I/O lines—A single clock wire can contaminate dozens of other lines by crosstalk.

- Always *pair* a signal trace with its return trace or, better, with the ground plane.

- When line becomes electrically long, implement impedance matching.

- For noise elimination, the best techniques are, in Increasing order of efficiency:
  —Wire-wrapped backplanes with a ground plane
  —double sided PCB, with a ground plane on one side
  —Multilayer boards

4   Power Supplies

Basically there are two types of power supplies: *linear regulators* (LPS) and *switched mode power supplies* (SMPS). Each one can be mounted after a normal stepdown transformer, a Faraday-shielded transformer or a ferro-resonant transformer.

The line and load regulation properties, including the dynamic response to rapid load change are distinct from EMI and are not addressed here.

Linear power supplies are relatively noise free and require less precaution. However, since they are relatively *transparent* to ac transients, some filtering is required. In this case, the ac mains filter will be the most efficient if located at the machine input (Fig. 4.1a).

Switched mode power supplies are noisy by nature since they generate harmonics up to 50 or 100 times their basic switching frequency. To avoid pollution of the entire internal wiring of the machine, a first step of filtering has to be achieved directly at the SMPS input (Fig. 4.1b). Figure 4.1c shows the principal modes of noise generation in SMPS.

4.1   Packaging

Up to $\simeq$ 50-100 watts, power supplies, especially SMPS, are generally packaged on pluggable PCB's. Above this rating, they are generally a hybrid of PCB and hard-wired assembly, in a metal frame. Most of the principles discussed in Sec. 2 apply.

- Route every hot wire with its 0V return (no loop surface).

- On harnessed assemblies, twist every hot wire with its return, keep wires as *short* as possible.

- Control, especially in SMPS, the loop area between the high voltage input capacitors, the switching transistors and the transformer's primary. This loop should be kept physically as *small* as possible.

- Use capacitor decoupling on board pins (differential mode) or feed-through capacitors (common-mode) must be mounted on the capacitors.

- Keep copper planes as large as possible. This decreases ripple and HF noise and is also cheaper (see Fig. 4.2).

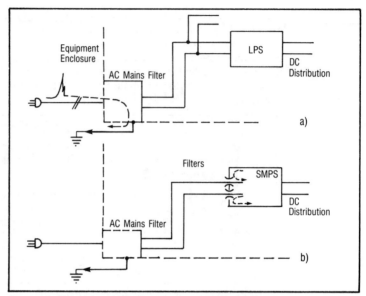

Figure 4.1—Principles of Filtering Linear and SM Power Supplies.

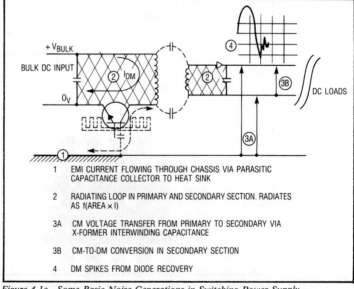

1   EMI CURRENT FLOWING THROUGH CHASSIS VIA PARASITIC
    CAPACITANCE COLLECTOR TO HEAT SINK

2   RADIATING LOOP IN PRIMARY AND SECONDARY SECTION. RADIATES
    AS f(AREA × I)

3A CM VOLTAGE TRANSFER FROM PRIMARY TO SECONDARY VIA
    X-FORMER INTERWINDING CAPACITANCE

3B CM-TO-DM CONVERSION IN SECONDARY SECTION

4   DM SPIKES FROM DIODE RECOVERY

Figure 4.1c—Some Basic Noise Generations in Switching Power Supply.

For PC cards which are not entirely Power Supply cards, but a mix of bulky, large current and low-level electronics, it is good practice to *leave* copper on all areas which have not been used for traces. Such planes can be on the component side and connected to the ground bus, or on the non-component side. In this case, the plane should be broken into a ground grid (Fig. 4.3) with about 50% voids to preclude flow-soldering problems.

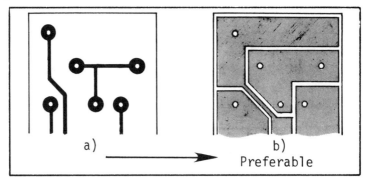

Figure 4.2—Recommended Layout for Power Printed Circuit.

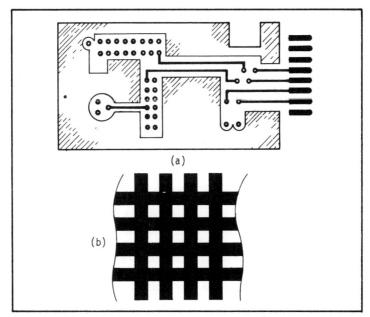

Figure 4.3—Copper Plane on Component Side a) and on Non-Component Side b). Grid is to Avoid Wave Soldering Problems Without Compromising the Low-Impedance Plane Concept.

4.3

- Use snubbers (RC network) with very short leads across the rectifiers terminals to damp HF oscillations.

- Use ferrite beads between transformer leads and diodes to damp HF oscillations.

- Select diodes with minimal (soft) recovery spikes.

- If the transistor heat-sink is small enough to be packaged onto the PC board, connect it to the collector (case) and keep it as far as possible from the metallic housing. It is best to leave some copper foil just underneath (not touching) the heat-sink, and connected to the dc input low.

- If the transistor heat-sink is large, it would be hazardous to let it at the dc input high (collector voltage). In that case, it must be isolated from the transistor case, but a Faraday shield, electrically insulated (Fig. 4.4), can be used to decouple HF leakages to the dc input 0 volt rather than let them pollute the ac input.

- Select a HF transformer with a low primary-to-secondary parasitic capacitance (split bobbin type, or toroidal) or with an integrated electrostatic (Faraday) shield.

- To decrease magetic flux leakage, use a magnetic shield (closed ring) around the whole transformer.

4.2 Filtering and Shielding at the Power Supply Level

Switched mode power supplies generate differential (phase-to-neutral) and common-mode (line-to-ground) noise. To attenuate this noise before it radiates into the entire equipment, it is recommended that the first step of filtering be implemented at the SMPS input level. Not untypically, an unfiltered switcher generates conducted EMI 40 to 60 dB above the typical FCC/CISPR/VDE limits. Once a suitable filter has been selected or designed, the key to filtering success is lead routing and filter location. This means mounting the filter components *as close* as possible to the power supply input terminals, and separating EMI conducting leads from regulated dc and sensing leads (Figs. 4.5a and b).

Although a shield is not a *must*, a little money invested in a perforated steel or aluminum shield around the SMPS can prevent noise problems at the equipment cabling level. The shield should enclose the whole PS block and be welded or fastened with screws at frequent intervals, every 5 cm, for instance.

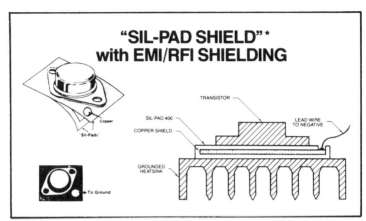

Figure 4.4—"Sil-Pad Shield" with EMI/RFI Shielding.

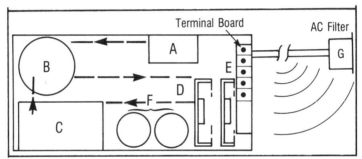

Figure 4.5a—Poor Layout of SMPS: Unfiltered ac input between PS block and filter G, radiates in the rest of the device. Primary diode A and electrolytic capacitor B form a large pick-up loop. Capacitor B to Xformer C and switch transistor D form a large radiating loop. Output ripple filter F and diodes E will pick-up switching harmonics.

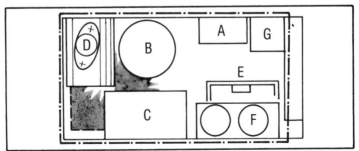

Figure 4.5b—Better Layout: ac Input is Cleaned-Up by Filter G Right at the PS Interface before ac wiring pollutes all the device. B, C, and D have been packed closely such that the HF switching loop is minimal. The dc output diodes E and ripple filter F have also been relocated away from the HF loops. A large copper plane is kept under BCD, as a common bulk dc (rectified ac) return. It also helps decoupling heat-sink noise before it goes to chassis. A shield is also suggested enclosing the entire PS.

Summary

- Separate EMI conducting leads (heavy switched currents) from *victim* leads (ac input, filtered dc output, sensing circuits, cooling fan leads).

- Keep EMI radiators (switching transistors and diodes leads, chokes) away from *victim* leads.

- On PCB mounted power-supplies, use large copper planes or grids for 0 volt return and bulk dc return, underneath the V+ traces.

- Use RC networks with ultra-short leads across rectifier diodes.

- On hard-wired power-supplies, twist hot with return wires, and keep leads short.

- For switching power-supplies, provide a first filtering at the power module level.

- Power supplies generate locally strong magnetic fields which are difficult to shield. If necessary, use a perforated aluminum or steel enclosure, bonded by overlapping and shielding at least five sides (the sixth side being the ground plane).

5 Internal Wiring and Packaging

Once the building blocks have been designed to be EMI free, it must be insured that intra-equipment wiring will not *induce* or *pick-up* EMI internally (self-jamming) or externally (susceptibility to ambients, or violation of FCC/CISPR/VDE/Military regulations).

To avoid inter-cable EMI coupling (crosstalk), one must identify, *at early design stages*, the various *cable families* , and designate their respective routing. For example:

- Category (1) ac power cables—Noise carriers
- Category (2)* dc distribution—Noise carriers and/or victims
- Category (3) signal and logic cables—Victims
  (a) Analog, low-level signals
  (b) Digital signals

5.1 Routing

- Category (1)—route along frame members and bottom of the machine/equipment,
- Category (2)—route along frame members and sheet metal plates, but separate from (1) (avoid *open space hanging*),
- Category (3)—route far from (1) and (2).

As a general rule, cables from subcategory (3b), carrying digital signals, should be spaced 2.5 cm (1 ″) from Category (1) for every 1 meter of their possible parallel run.

This separation will guarantee about 60 to 80 dB of isolation to frequencies as high as 10 MHz, i.e., a fast 500 volts transient of 30 nanosec rise time will not induce more than 50 to 500 millivolts, which is below the normal threshold for sensitivity of most of the logic families.

For cables from subcategory (3a), (depending upon the sensitivity of the circuits with which they interconnect), a spacing of 25 cm (10 ″) from category (1) for every meter of parallel run from typical power line transients is required to protect an analog circuit having 10 mV sensitivity.

---

*Signal wires from relays, circuit breakers, thermal switches, etc., fall in category (2).

Remember that power wiring not only carries 50/60 Hz voltages, but also has associated line spikes which couple strongly to nearby victim wiring. For example:

> If a packaging constraint forces analog signal cables to be run parallel to ac cables over a distance of 0.3 meter (1 foot), a separation of 25 cm × 0.3 = 7.5 cm (3 inches) should be provided.

Digital cabling (3b) can in turn be a noise carrier for more susceptible wiring like (3a). However, considering the low levels involved, it is a sufficient practice not to lace them together in the same harness. In all cases, at intersections, make right angle runs.

5.2   EMI Protection of Logic/Signal Cabling Category (3)

At this point, it will be useful to distinguish between the kinds of noises generated by *differential-mode* and *common-mode*.

Figure 5.1 shows that differential current I_{DM} is the *normal* useful (symmetric) current flowing to and from the load. A corresponding differential voltage can be measured wire-to-wire. The common-mode current I_{cm} (asymmetric) flows in both wires in the *same direction* at the same time. The corresponding common-mode voltage V_{CM} cannot be measured wire-to-wire, but it can be measured wire-to-ground.

To reduce EMI coupling from other cables, and outside EMI ambients as well, in all cases, each signal wire should have *its own independent return* running closely to it (no loop area, no common impedance return shared with any other signals). The four principal kinds of signal wiring are:

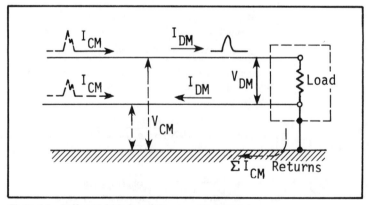

Figure 5.1—Differential Mode and Common Mode Noise.

Flat Cable and Ribbon

Each wire is surrounded by 1 or 2 ground wires equivalent to a shield as shown in Fig. 5.3b.

Although for cost saving reasons, some designers use only *one single return* in a ribbon cable, this is *poor practice* because the signal wire at the opposite edge can *radiate* and/or *pick-up* significant noise due to the width of the circuit loop (25 to 50 mm). Also, an alternate signal-ground-signal arrangement will reduce crosstalk between wires. Figure 5.2 gives the crosstalk for 1 meter of standard flat cable with alternate grounds.

Another risk of crosstalk with flat cables occurs when they are stacked above each other (Fig. 5.3c). In this case, alternate grounds do not help very much and the only solution is interposition of a spacer (about the same thickness as one cable) or a shield (Fig. 5.3d).

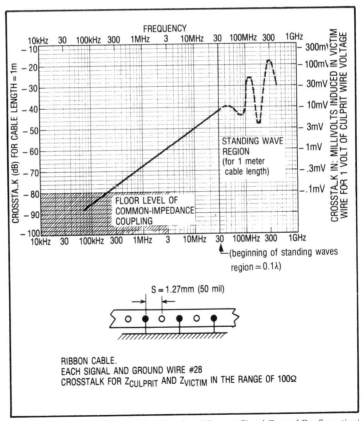

Figure 5.2—Flat Cable Wire-to-Wire Coupling (Alternate Signal-Ground Configuration).

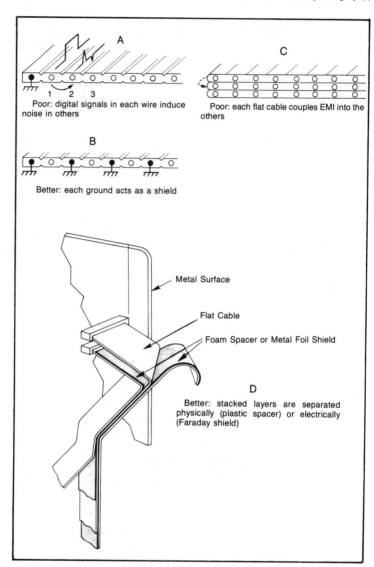

Figure 5.3—Flat Cable Spacing to Avoid Impedance Proximity Effects. (Courtesy of DEC).

Twisted Pair

Each wire runs with its return wire: very efficient against differential mode noise; inefficient against common mode noise.

Coaxial

The shield serves as 0V common return (Low Z). Connect the shield to 0V dc at *both ends.*

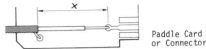

Paddle Card
or Connector

Stripped portion (X) may ruin the shield effect if it is too long. Disadvantage: the 0V surrounding the center wire may be disturbed by radiated or conducted noise.

Shielded Twisted Pair

Very efficient against:

- differential-mode noise (twisting)
- common-mode noise (shield)

For *low frequency* and high susceptibility, connect the shield to *Frame Ground* at one end only (receiving side unless there are other constraints).

Low frequency here means when the cable is *electrically short*, i.e., less than about 1/20 of the EMI wave length. For example, a 10 meter shield is short compared to a 1 MHz EMI problem (λ of 1 MHz = 300 meters). Given that condition, every point on the shield can be considered to be at about the same potential as its grounded end.

For higher frequencies, the ungrounded end of the shield can become so noisy that it couples EMI voltage into the box, at cable entry point, so it is better to connect both ends of the shield to frame ground, *at box entry.*

In all cases, connect unused wire ends to 0V or to a dummy load (never floating). Connect magnetic head cases and connector housings to *Frame Ground.*

In extreme cases (very high frequency transients, electrostatic discharge) install ferrite suppressors around the cable (Fig. 5.4). Ferrites work both by the added series inductance and equivalent resistance and start to be efficient above a few MHz. They behave like an added resistor which would *show up* for noise only, with values ranging from 1 MHz to 100 MHz of about 40 ohms for (a) and (b) and for an outside diameter of .3 cm and a length of .6 cm, and about 150 ohms for (c) and type (d) which is a special version for large conductors.

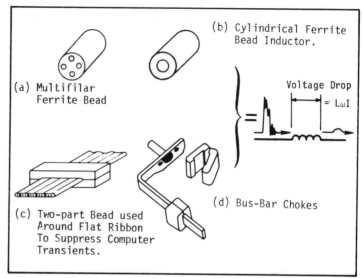

Figure 5.4—Typical Common Mode Suppression Ferrites.

5.3   Impedance of Discrete Wires and Jumpers

Table 5.1 gives the total impedance (resistance plus inductance) of large, medium and small wire gages for several lengths and frequencies. These values can be used to compute rapidly the voltage drop in conductors, especially for high frequency current.

For instance, if the instantaneous load change of a PC board is about 300mA in 100 nanosec (corresponding to a frequency of $\lambda/\pi\tau_r = 3$ MHz) and the dc voltage is supplied from the power supply regulator to the board pins by 30 cm of 2.5 mm wire (AWG #10); interpolation at 3 MHz shows an impedance of about 7 ohms, causing an instantaneous drop of $7 \times 0.3 = 2.1$ volts one-way. This is, of course, prohibitive since the power supply regulator, even with remote sensing, cannot *follow-up* such a rapid change. This is why a capacitive tank must be provided at the PCB connector (see Sec. 2.5), or a low inductance distribution between power supply and PCB has to be designed. One can see that increasing the size from AWG #10 (2.59 mm) to AWG #2 (6.54 mm) would not help very much, because the impedance is dominated by the self-inductance of the wire.

Another application of Table 5.1 is to check the efficiency of grounding jumpers and pigtails. If a shield is terminated to chassis by a 10 cm piece of AWG #22 (0.6 mm), this will be good enough grounding tech-

Table 5.1—Impedance of Straight Circular Copper Wires.

FREQ.	AWG#-2, D=6.54mm				AWG#-10, D=2.59mm				AWG#22, D=.64mm			
	ℓ=1cm	ℓ=10cm	ℓ=1m	ℓ=10m	ℓ=1cm	ℓ=10cm	ℓ=1m	ℓ=10m	ℓ=1cm	ℓ=10cm	ℓ=1m	ℓ=10m
10Hz	5.13µ	51.4µ	517µ	5.22m	32.7µ	327µ	3.28m	32.8m	529µ	5.29m	52.9m	529m
50Hz	5.20µ	55.5µ	624µ	7.16m	32.8µ	392µ	3.30m	33.2m	530µ	5.30m	53.0m	530m
100Hz	5.41µ	66.7µ	877µ	11.2m	32.9µ	332µ	3.38m	34.6m	530µ	5.30m	53.0m	530m
300Hz	7.32µ	137µ	2.19m	30.4m	33.7µ	365µ	4.11m	46.9m	530µ	5.30m	53.0m	531m
1kHz	18.1µ	429µ	7.14m	100m	42.2µ	632µ	8.91m	116m	531µ	5.34m	53.9m	545m
3kHz	52.5µ	1.28m	21.3m	300m	86.3µ	1.65m	25.0m	336m	545µ	5.71m	60.9m	656m
10kHz	174µ	4.26m	71.2m	1.00Ω	268µ	5.41m	82.9m	1.11Ω	681µ	8.89m	113m	1.39Ω
30kHz	523µ	12.8m	213m	3.00Ω	799µ	16.2m	248m	3.35Ω	1.39m	22.0m	305m	3.91Ω
100kHz	1.74m	42.6m	712m	10.0Ω	2.66m	54.0m	828m	11.1Ω	4.31m	71.6m	1.00Ω	12.9Ω
300kHz	5.23m	128m	2.13Ω	30.0Ω	7.98m	162m	2.48Ω	33.5Ω	12.8m	214m	3.01Ω	38.7Ω
1MHz	17.4m	425m	7.12Ω	100Ω	26.6m	540m	8.28Ω	111Ω	42.8m	714m	10.0Ω	129Ω
3MHz	52.3m	1.28Ω	21.3Ω	300Ω	79.8m	1.62Ω	24.8Ω	335Ω	128m	2.14Ω	30.1Ω	387Ω
10MHz	174m	4.26Ω	71.2Ω		266m	5.40Ω	82.8Ω		428m	7.14Ω	100Ω	1.29kΩ
30MHz	523m	12.8Ω	213Ω		798m	16.2Ω	248Ω		1.28Ω	21.4Ω	301Ω	3.87kΩ
100MHz	1.74Ω	42.6Ω			2.66Ω	54.0Ω			4.28Ω	71.4Ω	1.00kΩ	12.9kΩ
300MHz	5.23Ω	128Ω			7.98Ω	162Ω			12.8Ω	214Ω	3.01kΩ	38.7kΩ

```
*   AWG = American Wire Gage
    D   = wire diameter in mm
    ℓ   = wire length in cm or m          ██  Non-Valid Region
    µ   = microhms                            for which ℓ ≥ λ/4
    m   = milliohms
    Ω   = ohms
```

nique for audio frequencies (at 1 kHz, the wire presents 5.3 milliohms) but a very poor one at an EMI frequency of 100 MHz where it represents 71.4 ohms, i.e., it will be as if the shield was not grounded at all!

Figure 5.5 shows some typical electrical/electro-mechanical sources of *internal EMI* and the associated remedies.

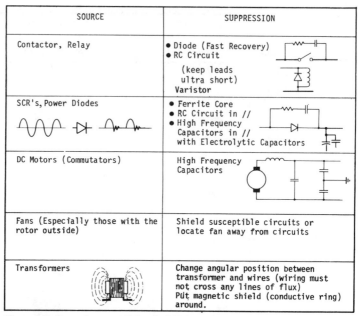

SOURCE	SUPPRESSION

Contactor, Relay	• Diode (Fast Recovery)
	• RC Circuit
	
	  (keep leads
	  ultra short)
	  Varistor

SCR's, Power Diodes	• Ferrite Core
	• RC Circuit in //
	• High Frequency
	  Capacitors in //
	  with Electrolytic Capacitors

DC Motors (Commutators)	High Frequency Capacitors
Fans (Especially those with the rotor outside)	Shield susceptible circuits or locate fan away from circuits
Transformers	Change angular position between transformer and wires (wiring must not cross any lines of flux) Put magnetic shield (conductive ring) around.

Figure 5.5—Some Sources of Electrical Noise (Internal).

5.4   Grounding Scheme

Regardless of the product or equipment being worked upon, whether it is a small home device or a large industrial system, it is *mandatory that the grounding scheme be determined and understood.* While grounding techniques may solve some EMI problems, ironically many EMI troubles occur because of uncontrolled grounding configurations which create deliberate or *ghost* ground loops. There are two main types of grounding options: *centralized* (single-point) or *distributed* (multi-point). As long as wiring distances are less than $\lambda/10$ at EMI frequency (refer to Sec. 6.1, chapter 6), the single-point (star) ground (see Fig. 5.6) is the most achievable and compatible with other constraints. Beware of the dramatic increase in impedance of regular wires when frequency and length increase (Table 5.1). The main rule is to eliminate any 0volt-to-chassis loops, which are the most troublesome. It also avoids the ground return current of one building block to flow through another block return wire, and possibly a build-up of some noisy voltage drops. Therefore, each building block has its 0V floated from the box, and the box itself hard-wired to the main terminal of the machine/equipment.

When the equipment has *internal noise sources* (as in Fig. 5.5) or is *insufficiently shielded,* the internal grounding scheme becomes crucial. It was said above that *single-point* (star) grounding is preferable. Unfortunately, when EMI frequencies become very high (VHF, UHF, radar, fast transients and ESD), the *single-point concept becomes a utopia* because:

a) grounding conductors become too impedant.

b) *floated* circuits become randomly grounded by their own parasitic capacitance to ground, which acts as a short.

In this case, the solution is:

- to block parasitic ground loop current circulation with ferrites (see Fig. 5.4), and/or

- decouple each PCB zero volt to ground *AT THE PCB INPUT CONNECTOR* by a small capacitance (short leads or feed-thru) in a similar manner as that shown on Fig. 6.20, *the important thing being not to let the ground loop currents pollute the PCB.*

Figures 5.6 and 5.7 illustrate the single point ground approach and its variations.

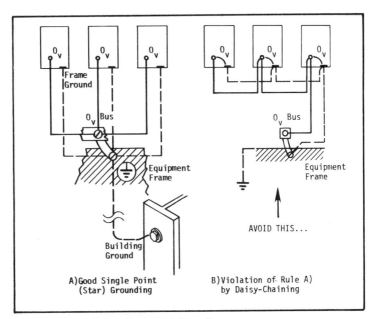

Figure 5.6—Typical Centralized (Star) Grounding.

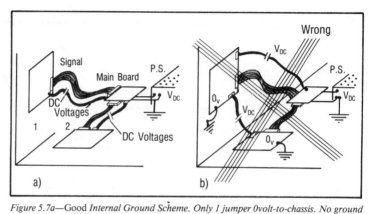

Figure 5.7a—Good Internal Ground Scheme. Only 1 jumper 0volt-to-chassis. No ground loops between 0vDC-signals chassis. If necessary, at connectors 1 and 2, a small decoupling capacitor to chassis can be installed to short induced transients to ground.
b—Poor Internal Ground Scheme. Several ground loops between signal, power distribution and chassis.

Summary

- To avoid contamination between wires, cabling must be classified in families, which will be routed separately:
  - —ac power
  - —dc power
  - —digital logic
  - —low level signals

- Noise pick-up can also take place between cables and chassis. Try to keep cables near a metal plane.

- Grounding *is* an electrical function and must be *designed* as seriously as any active circuit.

- A unique connection of the zero-volt to chassis (single point ground) is a good insurance against noise. However at high-frequency, its advantage may disappear and other techniques are required.

6   Final Box Design

An *ideal enclosure* should act as a *continuously closed conductive envelope* in order to prevent outside fields from penetrating equipment and to prevent internally generated noises from escaping the enclosure. Such an envelope also protects from ESD and provides a conductive media to bond the internal cable screens or component shields (Fig. 6.1). Unfortunately, an *ideal box* is never achieved, because of ventilation openings, maintenance panels and doors, cover seams, cable-through holes, and connectors. However, for practical considerations in designing a box, note the following:

- try to keep the number and sizes of *openings* (sides, top, bottom) to the *minimum* compatible with their functions (Figs. 6.2. and 6.3).

- cover ventilation openings or slots with *perforated grids* (1 mm thick, 2 mm diameter holes).

- insure continuous electrical contact between grids and chassis (welding, or fastener spacing $\leq$ 10cm).

6.1   Main Housing: The Outer Barrier Against EMI

The equipment box can be the first, and sometimes the only, barrier against radiation EMI problems. Think of the surface of a box as if it were a continuously conductive envelope. Every discontinuity, due to a door seam, screw or hinged-panel joint and/or assembled members, must have good electrical bonding qualities. The following list summarizes

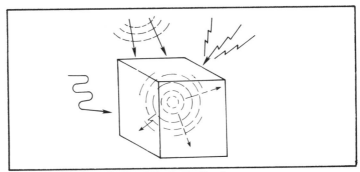

Figure 6.1—Continuously Closed Conductive Envelope.

Figure 6.2—Too Large, Unprotected Cable Entry.

Figure 6.3—Cable Entry Blinded and Cable Shields Grounded at Box Entry.

the solutions that may be considered in achieving good surface bonding, depending upon the severity of the EMI problem:

A) Painted frame→covers bonded by straps

B) Painted frame and riveted strips→covers with partial finger stocks

C) Frame with conductive paint→covers with conductive gasket

D) Entirely plated frame→covers with 100% finger stocks

Solution A only requires braided jumpers (Fig. 6.4). *Even though only one would seem to be sufficient to electrically ground the panel* to the frame, it is recommended that several jumpers be used and the spacings between them never exceed $\lambda/10$, where λ is the wavelength corresponding to the frequency where the potential EMI occurs. Remember that wavelength and frequency are related by:

$$\lambda_{meters} = \frac{300,000}{F_{kHz}}, \text{ therefore}$$

When:

$F = 1$ kHz	$\lambda = 300,000$ meters
$F = 1$ MHz	$\lambda = 300$ meters
$F = 30$ MHz	$\lambda = 10$ meters
$F = 100$ MHz	$\lambda = 3$ meters
$F = 300$ MHz	$\lambda = 1$ meter

If the EMI frequency is unknown, use grounding straps spaced not more than 20 cm (8 inches) apart. Do not place straps near sensitive items.

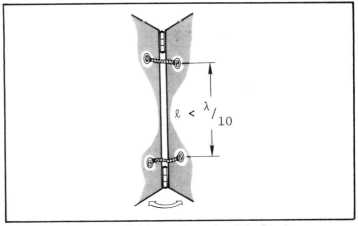

Figure 6.4—Solution A, Braided Jumpers Screwed on Paint Free Areas.

Solution B is an acceptable compromise which insures some continuity, not only on the hinged side, but on the entire perimeter of a panel.

Several types of finger stocks are available in two categories: the *low-pressure, knife-edge,* and the *medium-pressure spring contact* (Paragraph 6.2.3). Both types require adequate retention, proper flattening control and hinge adjustment (Fig. 6.5).

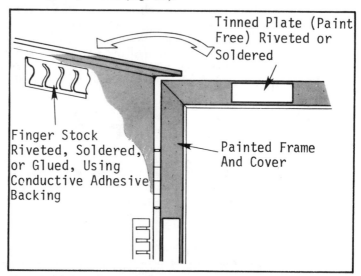

Figure 6.5—Solution B—To Maintain Shield Continuity with Painted Metal Box.

Solution C relies on a conductive coating over two mating surfaces. The coating acts as a paint to protect the metal against corrosion, and insures a good conductive media between each metal surface and the gasket. It also has the advantage of being effective in the case of plastic boxes.

Solution D is the most efficient since 100% of the seam becomes a very good conductive joint (Fig. 6.6). Besides its cost, it adds the need for a strong locking mechanism to insure good even pressure on all of the spring blades. This method is applicable to both rotating (hinged) or slide-mating surfaces.

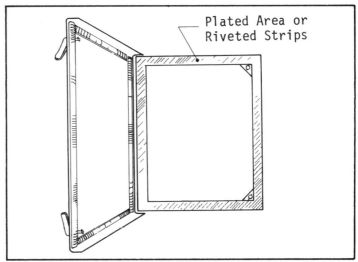

Figure 6.6—Solution D—100% Perimeter Coverage by Fingerstocks.

6.2   Shielding with Covers and Panels Seams

The efficiency of a housing as a shield can be totally negated by the shielding discontinuities at cover joints. So the design of covers is very critical in achieving shielding effectiveness (S.E.).

6.2.1   Cover Material

A metal cover is by far the best shielding that can be used. Steel is preferable to aluminum (or copper) due to good absorption loss provided its thickness is ≥ 1 mm. Below that thickness, aluminum or copper make equivalent or better shields, especially against close magnetic fields, because of their superior conductivity which gives good reflection losses for low frequencies where absorption is moderate.

Plastic covers provide no shielding whatsoever. Therefore, to achieve some attenuation, the following must be used:

- conductive plastic (conductive spray or mass inclusion of conductive particles). To be efficient in the normal 30 MHz-1000 MHz range, a surface resistance of less than 1 Ω/square is necessary, or

- internal shields over susceptible (PC boards, cable interfaces) or radiating (power supplies, CRT) areas. In extreme cases, special shields are needed: Nickel alloyed steel or Mu metal (its magnetic permeability μ_r is 60 to 80 times better than ordinary steel, up to about 100 kHz).

6.5

6.2.2 Cover Packaging

Provide overlapping of cover edges, even if there is no EMI gasket (see Fig. 6.7). *DO NOT PLACE TOO CLOSE TO COVERS,* and especially cover seams:

- Sensitive items = low-level logic, analog circuits, and high-speed logic.

- EMI sources = oscillators, transformers, relays, coils, and high-speed logic cards.

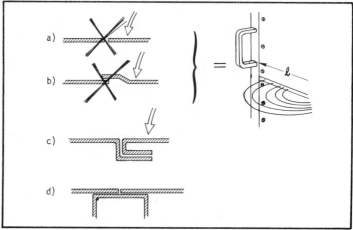

Figure 6.7—a) and b) shows edge mating of covers acting as a radiating slot. However good the shield effect was, it is merely reduced to the ratio of ℓ to λ/2, the half-wave length of the EMI field. In c) and d) the overlaps act as a capacitive coupling between the two covers and provides continuity.

6.2.3 Covers-to-Main Frame Bonding
(See also Box Shielding, Paragraph 6.1)

Always maintain a good electrical continuity between covers and main frame.

- with *STRAPS*—place strap far from sensitive items,

- with *FINGERSTOCKS*—partially or 100% require adequate retention, flattening (5-1.5 mm) and hinge adjustment,

Low Pressure   Medium Pressure (25 to 250g/cm)

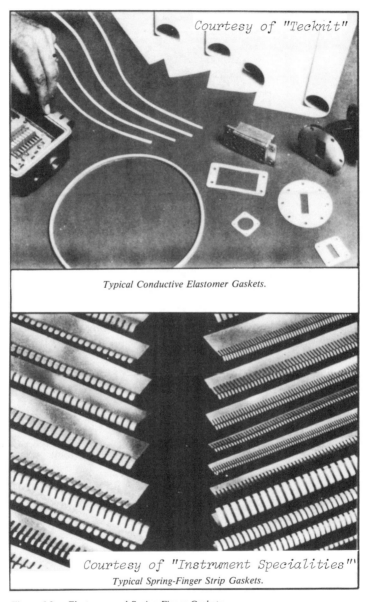

Typical Conductive Elastomer Gaskets.

Typical Spring-Finger Strip Gaskets.

Figure 6.8a—Elastomer and Spring-Finger Gaskets.

• with *EMI GASKET* + conductive paint, or plating (beware of gasket flattening) (Figs. 6.8a and b).

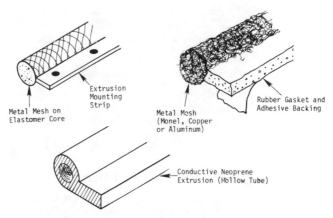

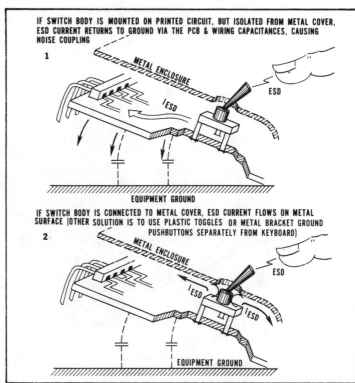

Figure 6.8b—Metallic Toggle-Switches, PCB Mounted.

6.3 Interface with Power Mains

Just as the shield prevents radiated EMI, the filter prevents conducted EMI from coming in or out of the equipment. However, the filter action cannot be disassociated from the overall shielding and the filter mounting has to be considered a part of the total shielding. Think of a filter as having a double role:

- first, it attenuates the *incoming* noise from other sources,

- second, it attenuates the noise *generated within the equipment itself.* This noise level is regulated by military specifications like MIL-STD-461B, or commercial specifications like FCC Parts 15 or 18, or VDE 871 and 875.

6.3.1 Selecting the Right Mains Filter

Filters must be carefully selected and the choice should not be based upon a vague belief in the manufacturer's catalog. A filter which has been good for one type of equipment may be inefficient for another type, or even too efficient. In this latter case, the filter may be more than what is needed in both cost and packaging aspect, providing, for example, a 1/1000 attenuation (60 dB) while the real need was to decrease the noise by a ratio of 1/10 (20 dB).

A proper selection of a power mains filter should consider:

- Highest nominal voltage,

- Highest, RMS input current (corresponding to the lowest voltage input tap setting, and the maximum optional features installed),

- Type of power supply—switching power supplies require an efficient filtering at low frequencies because of their high noise generation,

- Nature of electronic circuit inside of the equipment: low level analog circuits, and fast logic (as victims) and logic with significant transition current (as noise source) all require a well filtered power supply,

- Permissable leakage current to earth ground

Leakage current should comply with relevant safety requirements (National Electrical Code or U.L. in USA, or worldwide specifications like IEC.435) which generally require this current to be:

- less than 3.5 mA for EDP and office equipment with ground wire

- less than .5 mA for Class II equipment (double insulation)

As a general rule, it should be kept as low as possible.

Figure 6.9 is a reminder of what should be watched for in terms of filter data.

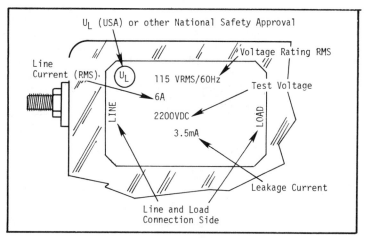

Figure 6.9—Example of Essential Filter Data.

6.3.2 Low Cost Filters

A relatively inexpensive and rugged filter (Fig. 6.10) made of a few discrete components, may be sufficient for less susceptible equipments, which have slow speed and circuits with good immunity, linear power-supply regulators with efficient output decoupling, or low-power devices. Also the performance of purchased filters may be upgraded by the addition of a capacitor between phase and neutral wires.

In the case of high power ac or dc, where large currents require an expensive choke, use feed-thru capacitors (Fig. 6.11).

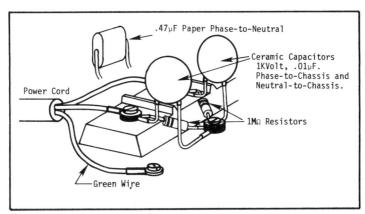

Figure 6.10—Home-Made Filter for Less Susceptible Machines.

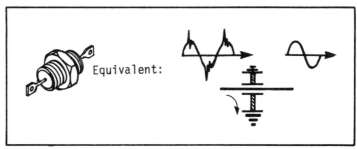

Figure 6.11—Feed-Through Capacitors.

6.3.3   Filter Location

Always put filters as close as possible to the power cord entry. Ideally, *the filter should be the first component the power cord encounters* when it passes through the equipment frame. Always keep the filtered output wiring away from the input wiring, and insure a perfect grounding of the filter case (paint-free, tinned areas). See Figs. 6.12 and 6.13.

Use High Frequency Caps (Ceramic, Polystyrene, Paper). Capacitor A traps differential noise, B traps common mode. Beware of lead length (keep as short as possible).

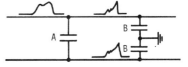

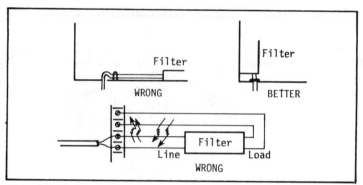

Figure 6.12—Do's and Don'ts *in Filter Mounting.*

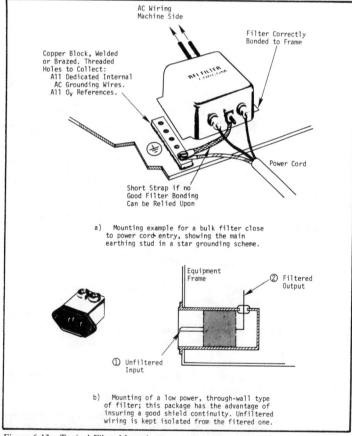

Figure 6.13—*Typical Filter Mountings.*

6.3.4 Transient Suppressors Other than Filters

Filters do not actually dissipate unwanted energy by their mode of operation, rather they repel undesired signals back toward the source (ac mains or ground). Other types of components can clamp large overvoltages that regular filters cannot handle. They are *varistors* and *gas-tube arrestors* (Fig. 6.14). These components are especially recommended for protection against *lightning-induced surges,* not only from power lines, but from any outdoor line or coaxial exposed to frequent lightning strokes, i.e., telephone/telecom, video or radio devices.

In Fig. 6.14a the gast tube practically shorts everything (spike and normal voltage) once its threshold voltage is reached, but it is slow to react.

As long as a surge voltage does not exceed the preset value, the gas tube is simply an open circuit. However, as soon as the firing threshold is reached, the gas tube performs as a closed switch, which short-circuits the surge. Once the surge is ended, the device stops to conduct and recovers its initial status.

In Fig. 6.14b the varistor *clamps* the voltage to a preset value. Varistors often require a low value resistance on the line before them to avoid destruction by too high surge currents.

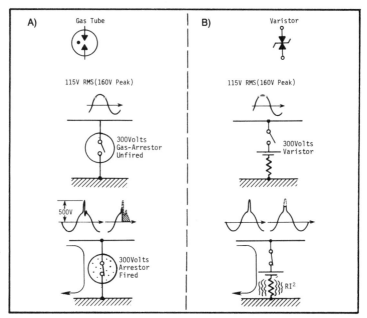

Figure 6.14—Basic Operation of Two Kinds of Transient Protectors: a) the gas tube practically shorts everything (spike and normal voltage) once its threshold voltage is reached; in b) the varistor clamps *the voltage to a preset value.*

6.3.5   Shielding of AC Cables

Shielding of an ac cable is not mandatory. It depends upon equipment operation, technology, noise susceptibility of logic, speed of logic, type of power supply and power mains ambient noise. If an efficient filter is required, or good low-impedance ground is necessary, shielding the power cord is a good and effective supplemental practice.

If shielded power cords are used, they should be of high quality (flexible, long life core). Safety aspects in some cases may prohibit their usage (for example, shielded power cords are not permitted on non-stationary equipment).

For Shield Termination of Power Cord (see also filter installation):

Machine side: Extend shield up to the line filter, which should be *closest* to the power cord entry hole and main earthing terminal. Connect the shield to the chassis ground with a 360° metal clamp (preferred to a jumper. See Fig. 6.15).

Plug side: If there is a good (or dedicated) earth wire, connect the shield to the ground pin along with the green (or green-yellow) wire (Fig. 6.16) or, better still, connect it with a 360° clamp to a metallic plug cap, when available. If a very noisy ground is suspected, it is better not to connect the shield to ground pin, plug side. Using a circular clamp, if the PVC jacket is to be fully inserted into the clamp, or strain relief, this can be accommodated by folding the shield back over the jacket (b). Grip type bushings like those used in electrical wiring (Thomas & Betts, etc.) are excellent for shield termination.

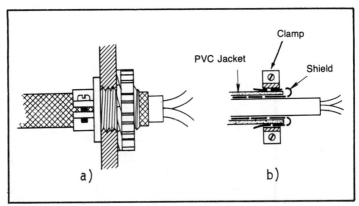

Figure 6.15—Correct Way to Terminate a Shielded Cable at Box Entry.

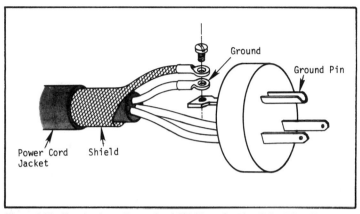

Figure 6.16—Terminating a Power Cord Shield on the Plug Side, When You Can Depend on a Good Earthing Wire.

6.4   Penetration and Immunization of Signal Interface Cables

At device entry holes, use separate locations for categories (1), (2) and (3) points of entry. Cable routings outside the equipment should also be controlled to avoid category mixes, whenever possible, and re-radiation.

On Fig. 6.17, the left side shows several mistakes: a long section of the power cord is running into the equipment until it reaches the filter. Then, I/O cables are running very close to this power cord. As a result, a) unfiltered power transients re-radiate into the equipment and pollute I/O cables creating transient logic/signal errors, b) high-speed signals from I/O can induce HF noise into the power cord *after* this one has been filtered and cause the unit to violate FCC, VDE or other EMI limits.

On Fig. 6.18 unshielded cables (A) or poorly grounded shields (B) penetrate the frame without crossing an integral metal barrier, then re-radiate.

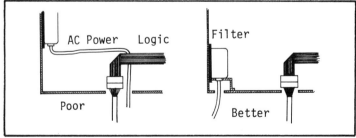

Figure 6.17—Cable Entries.

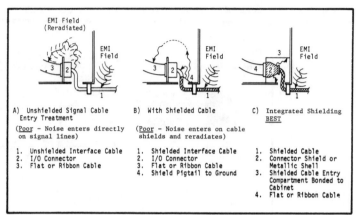

Figure 6.18—Do's and Don'ts for Cable Entry at Box Interface.

When the I/O cables are flat cables, should they be shielded or not? and how/where should the shield be connected?

If I/O cables connect only slow speed interface and the mother board I/O ports are well decoupled against high frequency (≥ 30 MHz) harmonics coming in or out, a shielded external cable is not necessary.

But if a superior shielding of the case was required and/or if the PCB design does not provide HF decoupling, an unshielded ribbon cable would be a severe *pick-up* (in terms of susceptibility) or *radiating* antenna (in terms of emission) because of its wide array of parallel pairs. In this case shielded flat cables are necessary. Referring to what was said in Sect. 5.2 for shielded pairs, and in contrast to coaxial cables, the shield here *is not an active conductor* but a protective barrier which must be in as much intimate contact as possible with the cabinet shield (our main protective barrier). Figure 6.19 A, B and C show what is desirable (A) and what is practically achievable (B and C) in terms of flat cable shield termination.

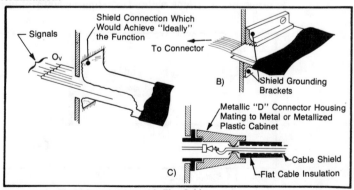

Figure 6.19—Shield Termination with Flat Cables.

A significant improvement can be obtained *at no cost,* just by giving some attention to the connector pin assignment, and subsequently to the wire arrangement into the ribbon or multipair cables. What we said for wiring families in Par. 5.1 also applies to external cabling. Always try to *pair* a current with its return. Unfortunately I/O connectors pin assignment is often dictated by Interface Standards where, in the past, very little (if any) attention has been given to EMI. Figure 6.20A is typical of the RS-232 (or CCITT-V24 for modems). In contrast, IEEE-488 provides a better pin assignment, noisewise (Fig. 6.20B).

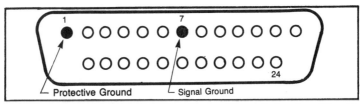

Figure 6.20 A—A Poor Arrangement, Giving Chances of Crosstalk, Impedance Mismatch and Radiation Problems.

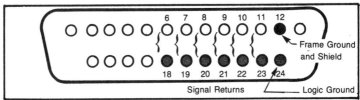

Figure 6.20 B—A Better Pin Arrangement, Showing Each Signal Paired with Its Own Return.

6.4.1   Special Types of Filtering for I/O Signal Cables

Filter-connectors and ceramic arrays can be used to clean signal lines directly at the equipment frontier (Figs. 6.21A and B). The rules for their location and mounting are similar to those for power mains filters. When selecting such filters, the designer should select a capacitor which will not significantly affect the normal (intentional) signal carried on the line, i.e., the cut-off frequency of the filter must be above the maximum useful signal bandwidth.

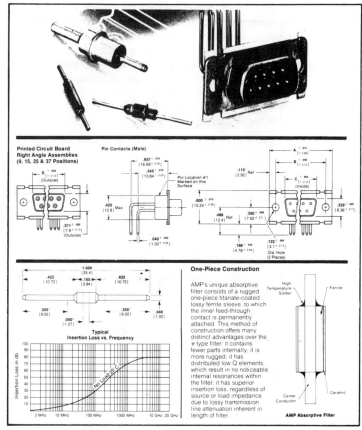

Printed Circuit Board Right Angle Assemblies (9, 15, 25 & 37 Positions)

E .005 [± 0.13] (Outside)

.311 .005 [7.9 ± 0.13] (Outside)

Pin Contacts (Male)

.657 .010 [16.69 ± 0.25]

.545 .010 [13.84 ± 0.25]

Pin Location #1 Marked on this Surface

.425 Max [10.8]

.040 .002 [1.02 ± 0.05]

.115 Ref [2.92]

.600 .015 [15.24 ± 0.38]

.488 Ref [12.4]

.300 .008 [7.62 ± 0.2]

.188 .025 [4.78 ± 0.64]

.122 .005 [3.1 ± 0.13] Dia. Hole (2 Places)

A .015 [± 0.38]
B .005 [± 0.13]
C .005 [± 0.13] (Inside)

.329 .005 [8.36 ± 0.13]

1.000 [25.4]

.422 [10.72]
.155 [3.94]
.422 [10.72]

.355 [9.02]
.050 [1.27]
.355 [9.02]
.040 [1.02]

Typical
Insertion Loss vs. Frequency

Insertion Loss in db: 100, 90, 80, 70, 60, 50, 40, 30, 20, 10

No Load/25° C.

2 MHz, 10 MHz, 100 MHz, 1000 MHz, 10 GHz, 20 GHz

One-Piece Construction

AMP's unique absorptive filter consists of a rugged one-piece titanate-coated lossy ferrite sleeve, to which the inner feed-through contact is permanently attached. This method of construction offers many distinct advantages over the π type filter: it contains fewer parts internally; it is more rugged; it has distributed low Q elements, which result in no noticeable internal resonances within the filter; it has superior insertion loss, regardless of source or load impedance, due to lossy transmission line attenuation inherent in length of filter.

High Temperature Solder
Ferrite
Center Conductor
Ceramic

AMP Absorptive Filter

Figure 6.21A—'20' Series Filtered AMP "Amplimite" Connectors.

6.18

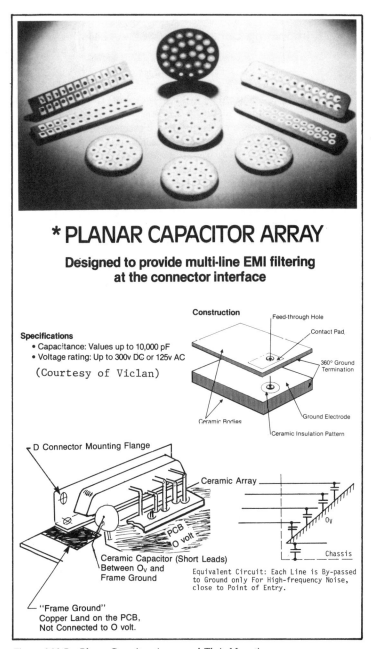

* PLANAR CAPACITOR ARRAY

Designed to provide multi-line EMI filtering at the connector interface

Specifications
- Capacitance: Values up to 10,000 pF
- Voltage rating: Up to 300v DC or 125v AC

(Courtesy of Viclan)

Construction

- Feed-through Hole
- Contact Pad
- 360° Ground Termination
- Ground Electrode
- Ceramic Insulation Pattern
- Ceramic Bodies

- D Connector Mounting Flange
- Ceramic Array
- PCB O volt
- Ceramic Capacitor (Short Leads) Between O_v and Frame Ground
- "Frame Ground" Copper Land on the PCB, Not Connected to O volt.

- O_v
- Chassis

Equivalent Circuit: Each Line is By-passed to Ground only For High-frequency Noise, close to Point of Entry.

Figure 6.21 B—Planar Capacitor Arrays and Their Mounting.

6.4.2 Improving Cabling Immunity to EMI

In addition to the above, a classical way to improve cable immunity (applied since the early times of telephony) is to use balanced isolation transformers which are available from the very low frequencies (audio applications) up to 20 MHz or more (Fig. 6.23). The basic improvement is shown in Fig. 6.22. Without EMI care (a), the noise interference developed between A and B creates a loop current which spoils the normal transmitted signal, especially if the transmission is unbalanced. Breaking the loop with isolation transformers (b), prevents I_{cm} from circulating since the transformer (ideally) should not process common-mode signals. In (c), the driver and receiver are balanced (they talk with + and − signals referred to 0volt). In (d), the unbalanced driver and receiver are balanced by using a BALUN (BALanced-UNbalanced) transformer. The BALUN has a shield to reduce the primary-to-secondary parasitic coupling, which has been grounded. A twisted pair is recommended to avoid field pick-up by the pair itself. Finally, in (e), total protection is achieved by adding a shield, which is grounded to the receiver side only (also to avoid circulating current in the shield).

For high speed digital interfaces, signal transformers are not preferred if there are many serial data streams, since they introduce a rise times skew; therefore, there are some inaccuracies in the setting *windows* of the link. So when isolation from ground is required (to avoid ground loops) balanced drivers and receivers are available. Be sure to select devices which have true symmetric outputs. Many times the author has seen so-called *balanced* links where there was as much current returning by the grounds as by the return wire of the pair! Even with average quality balanced drivers/receivers, it is not unusual to see, for 20 mA of pulse current, 2 mA (mainly high frequency harmonics) returning by the chassis ground. A simple way to see it is to clamp an RF current probe around the whole pair. Although the net current reading should be null if the transmission was perfectly differential, one will certainly see the high frequency glitches corresponding to the non-compensated current. This current, as small as it is, if flowing in the huge loop consisting of the cable, the box, and the ground is one of the strong contributors to FCC/VDE radiated EMI problems. Figure 6.24 shows balanced driver/receiver arrangements.

In addition to balancing, other techniques can be used to enhance rejection of very high frequency EMI, like optical-isolators or even fiber-optics.

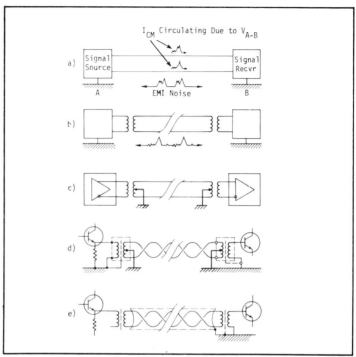

Figure 6.22—Using Balanced Transformers.

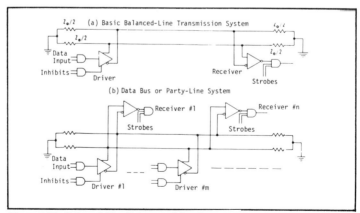

Figure 6.24—Balanced Line Drivers and Receivers.

Series 172   Courtesy of ADC Products

Courtesy of North Hills Electronics

Figure 6.23—Example of Commercial Types of Isolation Signal Transformers; Type a) is for audio applications (.2 to 4 kHz); Type b) is for fast clocks and video applications (10 Hz to 5 MHz). They provide common mode isolation from 40 dB to 60 dB, i.e., only 1% or .1% of the common mode noise appears on the Output Terminals.

6.5   Specially Hardened Equipment Housings

Finally, Figs. 6.25 and 6.26 show examples of super hardening. Figure 6.25 emphasizes maximum ESD (electrostatic discharge) immunity, while Fig. 6.26 shows a special emphasis on low emission levels (TEMPEST).

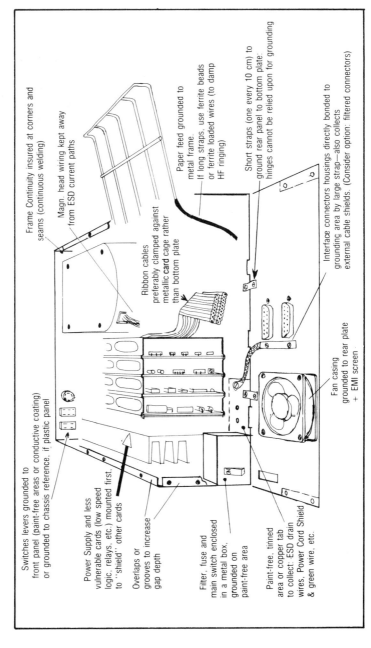

Figure 6.25—Fictitious Example Showing ESD Protection Measures.

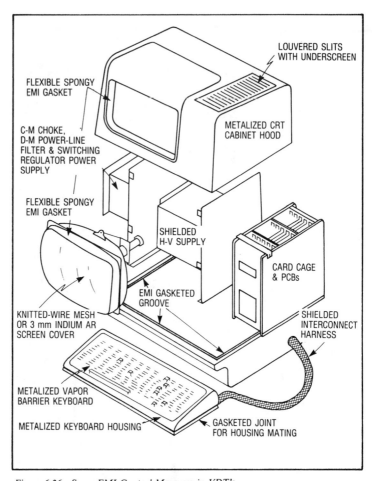

Figure 6.26—Some EMI Control Measures in VDT's.

Summary

- Equipment housing is the ultimate barrier (if everything else fails) against EMI pollution

- Until the last slot or hole has been taken care of, the best metal housing is a useless shield.

- Covers to mainframe bonding is essential in maintaining shielding integrity; the following choices exist:

Simplest and
Cheapest

A) Painted Frame ➤ Covers bonded by straps

B) Painted Frame ➤ Covers with finger
   + Riveted Strips   stocks on corre-
   (tin coating over   sponding surfaces
   nickel plating)   (10 to 50% of
                          perimeter)

C) Frame with con-   Covers with conductive paint ➤ ductive gasket
   or conductive,
   corrosion-free
   plating

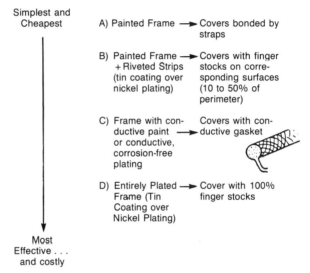

D) Entirely Plated ➤ Cover with 100%
   Frame (Tin   finger stocks
   Coating over
   Nickel Plating)

Most
Effective . . .
and costly

- Power line and I/O cable filtering are integral parts of the equipment shield. They must be mounted in such a manner that they do not degrade shield integrity but rather contribute to it.

7   Testing

When testing equipment for electromagnetic compatibility there are two important aspects to consider: *susceptibility* testing and *emission* testing. While susceptibility may be the most critical for user's satisfaction and the reliability of the product, it is *not,* with few exceptions, legally required at this time (1983). Therefore, manufacturers use their own internal specifications, or client specifications (for instance, MILITARY STANDARDS). Conversely, EMI emissions are rigidly regulated by INTERNATIONAL STANDARDS (CISPR recommendations) which have been conveyed through national laws like FCC, VDE, etc.

7.1   Emission Testing

Maximum emission levels have been set by an international commission, the CISPR, to protect radio communications from interference from all sorts of electrical noise sources. Since CISPR limits were generated by national committees of the CISPR, they are now in use or will be adopted for national limits in Europe, the USA and other major industrial countries. Small differences occur in some countries; however, if a product is designed to meet CISPR interference limits, it is likely that it will comply with limits of most countries.

Table 7.1 presents a summary of worldwide emission standards and regulations. For the moment (1983), the following electronic equipments are regulated:

- *INTENTIONAL RF SOURCES* (CISPR Publ. 11 or VDE 871): High frequency industrial equipment, ovens, welders, oscillators and, in general, any equipment which purposely generates RF energy. energy.

- *NON-INTENTIONAL RF SOURCES* (CISPR Publ. 14 or VDE 875): motors, switches, fluorescent lights, dimmers, etc., where the production of RF energy is fortuitous.

As it can be seen, nothing specifically addresses computer interference, but computers do, in fact, contain both intentional and non-intentional sources of EMI and many countries test them against both limits!

A CISPR document is in preparation which addresses only computing equipment. The emission limits specify the maximum conducted RF

Table 7.1—Electromagnetic Emission Standards of the CISPR Countries.

COUNTRY	IGNITION SYSTEMS	ISM	ELECTRIC APPLIANCES	RADIO AND TV	FLUORESCENT LAMPS AND LUMINARIES	SOLID STATE CONTROLS	COMPUTER PRODUCTS
CISPR	PUB 12	PUB 11	PUB 14	PUB 13	PUB 15		
Australia		DR 73117	AS 1044	AS 1053		AS 1054	
Austria		OVE F67/ 1957	OVE F60	OVE F60			
Belgium*	Royal Dec. 1960	Royal Dec. 1966	Royal Dec. 1968	Royal Dec. 1961			
Brazil							
Canada	SOR 75-629 CSA 108-4	SOR 163-455	CSA C 108.5.4			CSA22.4 VD. 1054	CSA C 108.8
Czech.**	CSN 34-2875	CSN 34-2865	CSN 34-2860	CSN 34-2870	CNS 34-2850		
Denmark*	MPWO 402	MPWO 44	MPWO 377	MPWO 14	MPWO 373	MPWO 213	
Finland	PUB T35-65	PUB T33-77	PUB T33-77	PUB T33-77	PUB T33-77	PUB T33-77	
France	NORME C91-100 & 91-103	NORME C91-100 & 91-102	NORME C91-100	C91.100 ADD 13	C91.100	C91.100	
E. Germany (GDR)***							
W. Germany	VDE0879	VDE0871	VDE0875	VDE0872	VDE0875	VDE0875	VDE0871
Israel							
Italy*	EEC DIR 72/		EEC DIR 245/CEE(9)		76.889		
Japan	Jap. PTT Recomm.	Radio Equip Reg. no. 65	Law No. 234	JRTC Recomm.	Law No. 234		
Netherlands*	Neth. Std. No. 531	NEN 10001	NEN 10001	NEN 10001	NEN 10015	NEN 10001	
Norway	Nor. Reg. for Motor Vehicles No. 43/63M	NEMKO 662.171 CIR. 22/74, 13/75	NEMKO 502.167 CIR. 23/74	NEMKO 661.77 CIR. 8/75	NEMKO 301.173 CIR. 21/74	NEMKO 665.168 CIR. 13/71	
Poland**	PN-70/ S-76005	PN-71/ E-06208	PN-70/ E-06008	PN-71/ T-05208	PN-76/PN-71/ E-06231	E-06218	
Romania	STAS 6048/4-71	STAS 6048/6-71	STAS 6048/7-71	STAS 6048/9-71	STAS 6048	STAS 6048/7-71	
S. Africa	Radio Reg. R2247	Radio Reg. R2247	Radio Reg. R2247	Radio Reg. R2247	Radio Reg. R2247	Radio Reg. R2247	
Spain	UNE 20509	UNE 20506	UNE 20507				
Sweden	SEN 471001	SEN 471002	SEN 471004 1006 & 1007	SEN 41007 & 471008		SEN 471003	SEN 471010
Switzerland*		ASE 1001					
USSR**	(Appears to use CISPR Limits) GOST 14777						
United Kingdom*	BS 833	BS 4809	BS800	BS 905	BS 5394 Part 1	BS 800 Part 3	
USA	SAEJ551C SAEJ1113	FCC Part 18		FCC Part 15			FCC Part 15J

Notes: The majority of industrial countries follow CISPR Recommendation in their national rules.
* Countries known to follow and are awaiting common market directives (EEC) implementing CISPR requirements.

** Eastern European countries follow mutual economic AID Council (COMECON) Standards.

voltage on power cords (Fig. 7.1) and the maximum radiated field at a given distance (Fig. 7.3). In some cases (small equipment, with only one power cord) the radiated field test is replaced by a measurement of the radiated energy picked-up by an absorbing clamp located in the power cord. For conducted noise, an artificial network (LISN) is used (Fig. 7.2).

For radiated tests (Fig. 7.4), the equipment is installed on a free-field test site, far from reflecting objects and the antenna height above ground is varied to adjust to the maximum emission levels.

Each country has its specific procedures to insure that manufacturers are delivering products which meet emission limits. Some require test and certification by a national laboratory (for example, the VDE in Germany) and some accept manufacturers' self-certification.

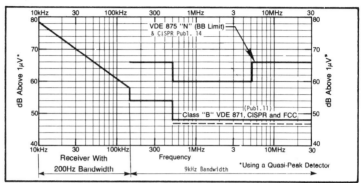

Figure 7.1—Typical Conducted Emission Limits Applicable to Computers. The VDE 875 limit addresses broadband noise while VDE 871 addresses narrowband (sharply tunable) harmonics.

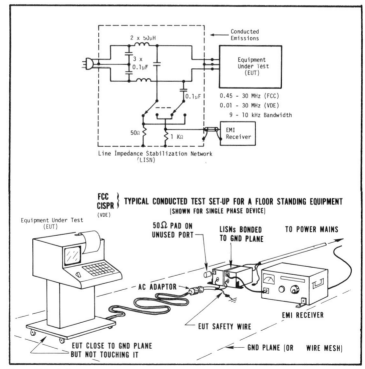

Figure 7.2—Schematic and Test Set-Up for Conducted EMI Testing of a Computing Device.

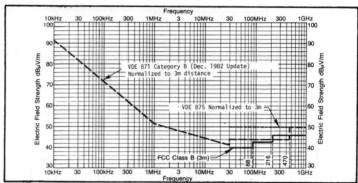

Figure 7.3—Typical Radiated Emission Limits Applicable to Computers. From 10 kHz to 30 MHz, the field is measured by a loop antenna, in 9 kHz bandwidth. Above 30 MHz, it is measured by a dipole, in 100 kHz bandwidth.

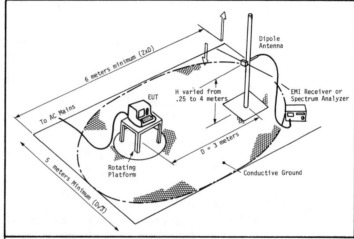

Figure 7.4—Typical Radiated Test Set-Up for Small Computers and Office Equipment.

7.2   Computers Emission Limits in the USA

The FCC, the US regulatory agency, has ruled on computers since 1981. Its approach is slightly different. The FCC considers two classes of computing equipment:

- Class A—computers for use only in industrial and commercial environments

- Class B—Computers marketed for use in residential environments.

Because of higher probabilities of proximity with a radio or TV listener, class B limits are 10 dB more severe than Class A and certification procedures are more stringent.

It is likely that the CISPR Standard on computer emission will be close to FCC A and B rules, since the FCC has worked closely with CISPR experts. Figure 7.5 shows conducted and radiated FCC limits.

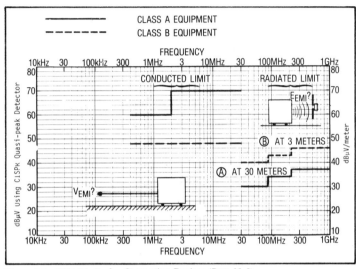

Figure 7.5—FCC Limits for Computing Devices (Part 15.J).

7.3 Susceptibility Testing

Since there is almost no legal obligation for a computer to be immune to EMI, each manufacturer uses its own in-house specifications. An example of what is commonly considered to be *reasonable* immunity is shown in Fig. 7.6. This corresponds to realistic worst case environments such as those described in Chapter 1.

- RADIATED E-FIELDS
  - 1V/m from 150kHz to 25MHz
  - 10V/m from 25MHz to 10GHz
- INDUCED MAGNETIC FIELDS
  - From 20 Amps at 60Hz into cabinets and interconnects cables
- ELECTROSTATIC DISCHARGES
  - 7500 Volts from 100pF through 1200 Ohms (up to 3 times this value for non-controlled environment)
- POWER LINES
  - ±1000 Volt 50 nsec transients over 360°: Differential (Phase to Neutral) and Common Mode (Phase to Ground)

Figure 7.6—Suggested Susceptibility Limits for Computers in Commercial Environments.

The induced magnetic field test is made by coiling about three turns of wire around the equipment frame and driving 20 amps through it to simulate the proximity of large ac currents.

The ESD test is probably the most powerful and immediately reveals weaknesses of the design and packaging. Some companies test with lower values of discharge resistance; for instance, 10,000 volts and 150 Ω resistance to simulate furniture discharge in addition to human body ESD.

Fig. 7.6B shows a practical set-up for an ESD test. Before the test, the operator selects all the points where a discharge can realistically be applied. The purpose of the test is to find at which ESD voltage errors start to appear. The criticality of these errors (for instance, are they recoverable by software?) is a criteria in deciding if the machine fails or meets the test.

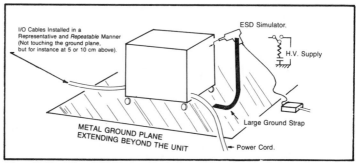

Figure 7.6 B—Direct ESD Testing. For indirect *ESD, when the device under test is entirely plastic, the discharge is made on a grounded vertical plate instead.*

7.4 Military Standards

For EMC, the most famous and worldwide adopted specifications are the MIL-STD-461 (limits) and 462 (test procedures) issed by the US Department of Defense. Military specifications are more complete and stringent in the sense that they address conducted and radiated *susceptibility* as well as *emission*, and at all frequencies from 30 Hz to 10 GHz.

The approach of MIL 461 for EMC testing is shown in Fig. 7.7. The categories of tests are organized as shown in the block diagram of Fig. 7.8. A two-digit code is used:

C = conducted   E = emission
R = radiated   S = susceptibility

A few examples of MIL-STD-461 are shown (Figs. 7.9 and 7.10). For instance, a certain type of equipment must not radiate more than 20 dBμV/m at one meter distance around 20 MHz and must be immune to 10 volts/m below 20 MHz.

Military specifications are often used as the criteria for the design of non-military equipment.

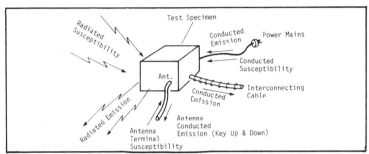

Figure 7.7—Conceptual Illustration of Interference and Susceptibility of Test Specimen.

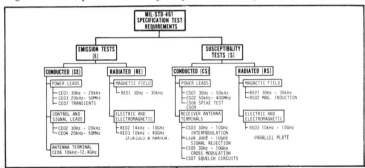

Figure 7.8—Organization Tree of MIL-STD-461 Test Specifications.

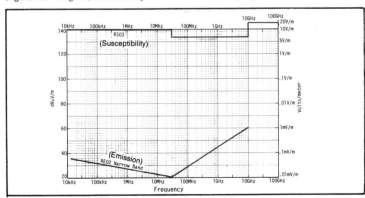

Figure 7.9—Example of Some Radiated MIL-461 Limits.

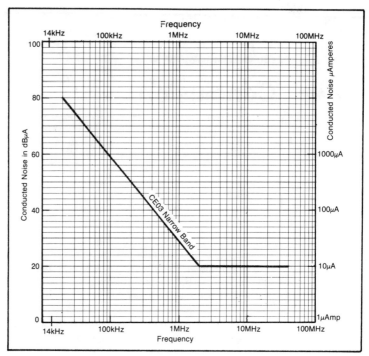

Figure 7.10—Example of MIL-461 Conducted Emission Limit.

8 Conclusion

Electromagnetic compatibility must be considered early in the design stages of new equipment. If it is ignored until EMI problems are encountered during testing or in the field, fixes become very expensive—primarily because the design is less flexible.

As a piece of equipment goes through the various developmental stages, i.e., initial design, prototype testing, shipment test and production, the choice of feasible changes decreases rapidly.

A noise problem on a printed circuit board, for example, can be solved at the layout stage for a relatively small cost. However, if it is dealt with at the motherboard level the cost could increase 10 times, or ultimately 100 times, if the box design will have to make up for the internal deficiencies. Figure 8.1 illustrates that EMC achieved at the design stage is a one-time cost, while EMI problems and fixes in the field can cost an enormous amount of money if engineering changes and/or retrofit are necessary.

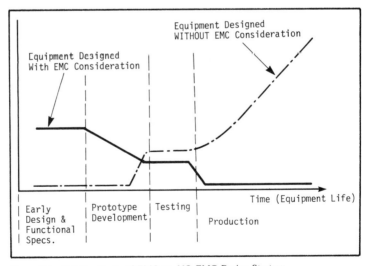

Figure 8.1—Relative Costs of EMC vs. NO EMC Design Strategy.

Appendix A
Frequency Spectrum of Digital Pulses

The purpose of digital equipment is to process time varying waveforms, generally having a value equal to 0 volt for logical "0" (or "false") and a few volts for logical "1" (or "true"). On the other hand, EMI Specifications (FCC, CISPR/VDE, MIL-STD 461, etc.) are defined in frequency domain, as are performances of filters and shielding materials. So, one way or another, time must be translated into frequency or vice versa.

Fourier Theory states that a periodic signal can be expressed in terms of a series of sine and cosine signals, at frequencies which are multiple integers of the pulses period. However, a problem appears: the FCC specifications range from 450 kHz to 1 GHz and the VDE specification ranges from 10 kHz to 1 GHz. If one were to take a complex time domain waveform and perform a rigorous Fourier analysis, to compute the amplitudes and phases of every harmonic from fundamental to #1,000 or #100,000, it could take days or weeks. Fortunately, some simplifications exist which, providing some assumptions are made, allow for a quick calculation process with acceptable results.

Therefore, the problem can be broken into two steps:

1) Identify the waveform and period of time varying signal.

2) Perform a time domain to frequency domain conversion so it can be compared to the specification limit, once the proper coupling coefficients have been applied.

Step (1) is relatively easy. Connect an oscilloscope to the source and then take a picture. Be sure that the bandwidth of the oscilloscope is large enough to reproduce the rise times of the logic family used, without distortion (use bandwidth $\geq 0.3/\tau_r$ as a rule of thumb). Then, approximate the time domain waveform by one of the following waveforms:

A. For Trapezoidal Waveform

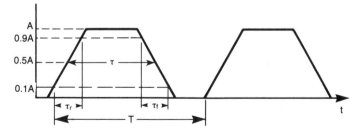

B. For Triangular (Isosceles) Pulses

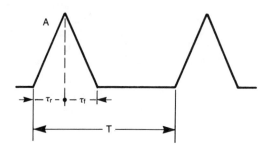

Once the waveform has approximated the shape shown on A or B, the following approximations are required to perform step (2).

—if $\tau_r \neq \tau_f$, only the smallest of the two will be considered
—only the envelope of the maximum amplitudes will be considered:

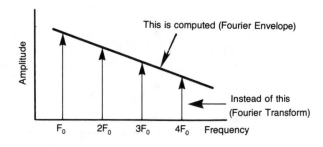

Frequency Domain Approximate Representation for Trapezoidal Waveform, A

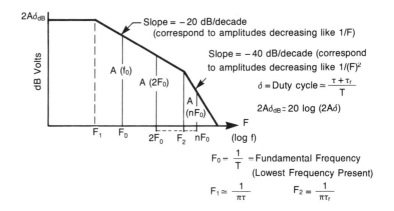

For a periodic waveform, the frequency spectrum is composed of discrete frequency components consisting of the fundamental (f_0) and integral multiples (harmonics) of f_0. The units of 2A are volts, millivolts, Amps, etc. If $\tau_r \neq \tau_f$, select the smallest of the two.

For Triangular Waveforms B)   Assuming $\tau_r \simeq \tau_f$

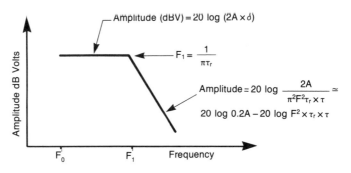

Note: $F_0 = 1/T$ can be greater than F.

To speed up the construction of the spectral profile, the nomogram of Fig. A1 can be used.

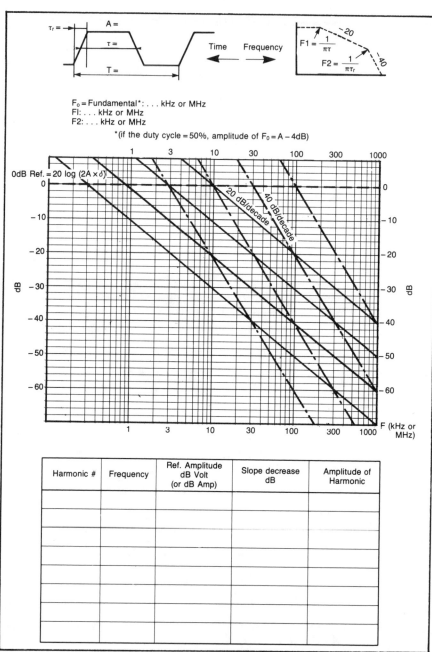

Figure A.1—Nomogram to Predict Pulse Train Spectrum.

A.4

The nomogram was constructed to provide an easy and fast approximation of the total spectrum occupied, as well as the amplitude of some typical (maximum) harmonics.

To understand how to use it, consider a clock signal having the following characteristics:

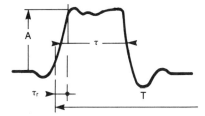

Voltage Amplitude = 4 volts
Rise time = 10 nanosec.
Period T = 100 nanosec.
Duty Cycle = 50%

The first thing to do is to identify the 3 key frequencies of such a spectrum. The fundamental, F_0 obviously 1/100 ns = 10 MHz.

The 1st corner frequency, $F_1 = \dfrac{1}{\pi\tau} = \dfrac{1}{\pi \times \dfrac{100}{2} \times 10^{-9}} \simeq 6 \text{ MHz}$

(Note that at this frequency, the spectrum has no component yet, but F1 is necessary to construct the envelope.)

The second corner frequency, $F_2 = \dfrac{1}{\pi\tau_r} = \dfrac{1}{\pi \times 10 \times 10^{-9}} \simeq 30 \text{ MHz}$

(Note how critical this frequency is, as it is related to the rise time. The shorter the rise time, the higher the spectral occupancy.)

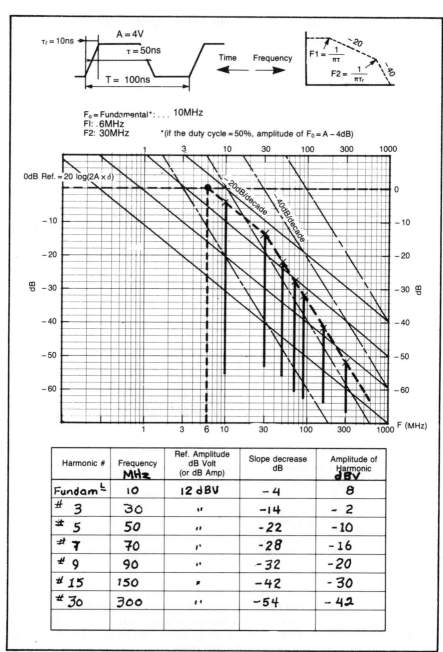

The figure shows a pulse train waveform with $\tau_r = 10$ns, $A = 4$V, $\tau = 50$ns, $T = 100$ns. Time ← | → Frequency. Spectral envelope with $F1 = \frac{1}{\pi\tau}$, $F2 = \frac{1}{\pi\tau_r}$, slopes -20 and -40.

F_o = Fundamental*: ... 10MHz
FI: .6MHz
F2: 30MHz   *(if the duty cycle = 50%, amplitude of $F_0 = A - 4$dB)

0dB Ref. = 20 log(2A × δ)

Harmonic #	Frequency MHz	Ref. Amplitude dB Volt (or dB Amp)	Slope decrease dB	Amplitude of Harmonic dBV
Fundam ᴸ	10	12 dBV	-4	8
# 3	30	"	-14	-2
# 5	50	"	-22	-10
# 7	70	"	-28	-16
# 9	90	"	-32	-20
# 15	150	"	-42	-30
# 30	300	"	-54	-42

Figure A.2—Nomogram to Predict Pulse Train Spectrum.

A.6

What remains is to calculate the starting amplitude of the reference line:

$$20 \log_{10} 2A \times \tau/T = 20 \log_{10} 2 \times 4 \text{ volts} \times \frac{50}{100} = 12 \text{ dB volt}$$

The frequency F_1 (6 MHz) is plotted on the top 0dB Ref, then a 20 dB/decade slope is drawn, using the parallel grids, until the frequency F2 (30 MHz) is encountered. From this point, a 40 dB/decade slope is drawn. The envelope has now been constructed: it is the locus of all maximum amplitudes. The form below the nomogram allows one to compute the amplitude of any significant harmonic in dB Volt. To find the amplitude in dBμV one should simply add 120 dB, since 1 volt $= 10^6 \mu V = 120 dB\mu V$.

A few clarifications are necessary:

Q: The envelope shows the locus of the maxima. What about the other harmonics?

A: With a simple 50% duty cycle, only odd harmonics exist, and they follow this envelope exactly.

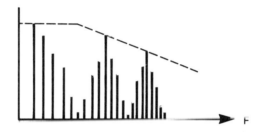

For smaller duty cycles, i.e., when the period becomes significantly long compared to the pulse duration, only a few harmonics in the series reach the maximum level. However, they are the harmonics which will most likely create the EMI problems, precisely because they have the highest amplitude. *Murphy's Law* (which in EMC has found the most impressive field of application), would say that if any susceptible circuit has some specially critical resonancy, this is exactly where the EMI sources will show their best.

Q: Should not the envelope show phase or polarity?

A: True. At every multiple of $1/\tau$, there is a 180° reversal due to the fact that harmonics follow a sine or cosine function of frequency. However, EMI receivers use to measure EMI emissions (for FCC or CISPR) and Spectrum Analyzers are insensitive to the phase and will display the absolute value.

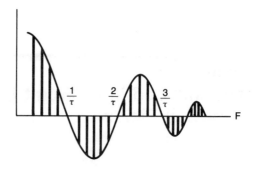

Q: When harmonics are closely packed together (i.e., the period is relatively long and there are many harmonics in a MHz interval), should they be added one way or another?

A: For computers, the majority of repetitive signals have repetition rates higher than 10 kHz. Switching power supplies, for instance, and using chopping rates of 20 kHz or more, and clock frequencies are always superior to a few hundred kHz.

Since the receivers used to measure EMI emissions have a bandwidth of 10 kHz for conducted EMI, and 100 kHz for radiated EMI, the noise will generally appear *narrowband*, i.e., *the receiver will only see one harmonic at a time within its resolution bandwidth.* However, it is true that in some situations (MIL-STD for instance), the broadband addition of spectral components should be considered and, in this case, the spectral amplitude is expressed in μVolts/kHz or μVolts/MHz. This topic would exceed the scope of our book. The reader will find more details on this subject in the following references.

References

1. Di Marzio, Alfred, *Graphical Solutions in Harmonics Analysis,* IEEE Transactions on Aerospace, September 1968.
2. Audone, Bruno, *Graphical Harmonics Analysis,* IEEE Transactions on EMC, May 1979.

Appendix B
Voltage Induced in a Circuit Loop by Ambient EMI Fields

Any time a circuit is placed in a time varying electromagnetic field, a voltage is induced in the circuit. This voltage increases with the size of the circuit, the frequency (or the rise speed) and amplitude of the field variation. This is how rotating electric generators function, how transformers function and how receiving radio antennas perform. The computer designer certainly did not plan to make an antenna or an alternator from his cables. However physics prevailed over what the engineer wanted or not and, if electronic circuits and cables are illuminated by EMI fields, undesired voltages will appear by magnetic or electric induction. Especially critical are the voltages induced in the unavoidable loops formed by cables and ground plane, or a wire and its return when they are not kept close to each other.

Common-mode coupling converts an ambient electric or magnetic field to a common-mode voltage into the loop area as shown in Fig. B.1. This voltage then acts as a potential EMI source to push current around the loop area which includes the victim cable. The resulting differential-mode voltage developed in the victim cable appears across the amplifier, or logic input terminals, to constitute the potential EMI threat.

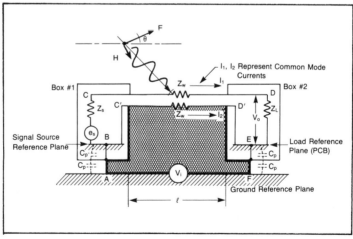

Figure B.1—Coupling of Ambient Fields into Cable-to-Ground Loop.

Ground loops are formed when two interconnected boxes are located near a ground plane or safety wire, whether or not they are connected. Thus, ground-loop impedances may be low or high at any frequency, but the induced common-mode voltage is independent of the loop impedance.

The term *ground* here is intended to imply a location or place to which any circuits, equipment or system potential may be referenced.

It may or may not include the earth, a *ground* plane, a safety wire, a cold-water pipe, etc. A ground loop, however, does convey the idea of some form of a closed loop, usually having a low impedance, perhaps at dc. Most engineers agree that a ground loop exists when two or more interconnected circuits, equipments or systems are connected to a common *ground* reference.

One way of looking at a ground loop or, more generally, a loop area, is to consider the evolution of a loop area shown in Figs. B.2-B.5. First, consider a cable or harness suspended in the air, well removed from the presence of any ground or earth. Figure B.1 shows such a horizontally deployed cable in the presence of a horizontal electric (E) or orthogonal magnetic (H) field. The cable is acting like an unintentional pickup antenna. For the presence of a horizontally polarized E-field, the open-circuit induced voltage, V, into the cable is defined:

$$V = \int_{0}^{\ell} E \cdot ds \text{ volts} \tag{B.1}$$

$$\simeq E\ell, \text{ for } \ell < < \lambda \tag{B.2}$$

where,

E   = electric-field strength in V/m
ds = small segment of wire length
ℓ = length of cable in meters
λ = wavelength corresponding to frequency of the E-field

The common-mode voltage, V, causes a cable conduction current to flow as shown in Fig. B.2. For a current to flow, there must be a closed loop. The return loop current, called displacement current, flows through an everpresent end-to-end cable capacitance. While this capacitance is distributed along the cable length, an equivalent bulk capacitance results in a definable loop area shaped like a football. This is generally referred to as the equivalent area (loop) of an antenna, even though the *cable antenna* appears to be physically one dimensional. The current will be very low at low frequency when $\ell < < \lambda$ since the capacitive reactance is very high.

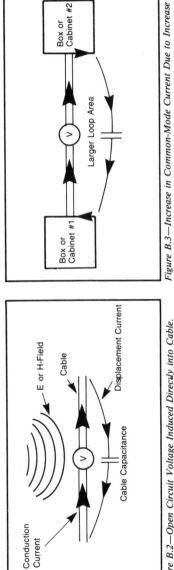

Figure B.2—Open Circuit Voltage Induced Directly into Cable.

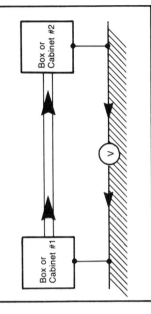

Figure B.3—Increase in Common-Mode Current Due to Increase in Capacitance.

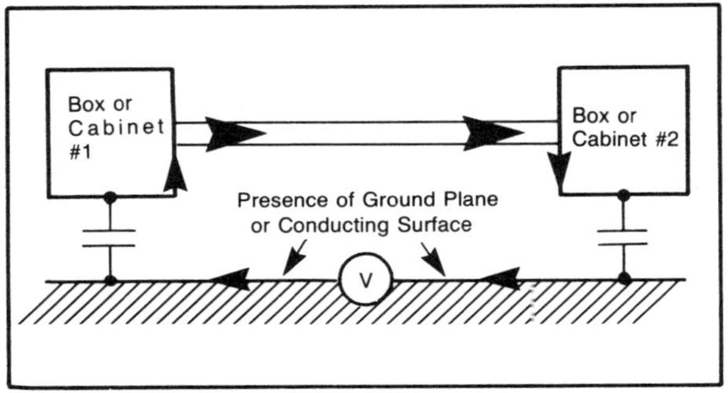

Figure B.4—Further Increase in Common-Mode Current and Definable Loop Area.

Figure B.5—Still Further Increase in C-M Current and Definable Loop Area.

When boxes, equipments, racks or consoles are connected to both ends of the *suspended cable antenna,* an increase in both the end-to-end cable capacitance (*top-hat* effect) and loop area results (Fig. B.3). Consequently, the induced common-mode voltage and current increase. The current increases at a greater rate, however, because of the presence of both a larger voltage (larger loop area) and a lower circuit impedance (higher capacitance).

In Fig. B.4, the *suspended* configuration has been brought down to a location near the presence of a ground plane, a safety wire or earth (hereafter, it will simply be called a conducting *ground*).

The capacitance between both ends of the cable has substantially increased as a result of the capacitance between both boxes to ground. The direct capacitance between both ends of the cable, per se (see Fig. B.2), is now small relative to that via the box-ground-box-route and the loop area is better defined. Thus, the induced common-mode voltage is more apparent and the common-mode current further increases due to the lower circuit impedance and increased capacitance).

In Fig. B.5, both boxes are now directly connected to ground. The loop area has not changed much. However, the common-mode current can increase substantially provided that: (1) the cable circuits inside each box are grounded to the box case (see earlier Fig. 2.3) or, (2) the cable is a coaxial line or shielded line with both ends of the braid or shield connected to the boxes.

Figure B.5 is an example of what most engineers would agree is a *ground loop.* However, it is also believed that most engineers would agree that Fig. B.4 is *not* an example of a ground loop since both boxes are not connected (direct hardwire or strap) to ground. Yet, the only significant difference is in the circuit impedance, not the loop area. Thus, both Figs. B.4 and B.5 are ground loops. At some frequencies, the circuit impedance of Fig. B.4 will be *lower* than that of Fig. B.5 because the circuit would have gone through series resonance (box-to-ground capacitance and cable inductance). The reader should now identify with the loop area and loop impedance separately, and not limit his thinking to a low-resistance, dc ground loop path.

As suggested above, not all cable-ground loop areas are well defined. Figure B.6 shows a well-defined loop area in which both boxes or cabinets are directly bonded to a metal decking. The length is simply the inside distance between the boxes. The equivalent cable height is computed by averaging different height samplings along the cable length.

In Fig. B.7, the common-mode loop area is harder to define. If one or both cabinets are floating (this violates electrical safety codes), capacitances are developed between the bottom of the cabinets and any nearby metal. Here, the RF *ground* may be reinforcing bars or mesh immersed in concrete below the cabinet casters. The shaded area in the figure suggests how the loop area may be calculated.

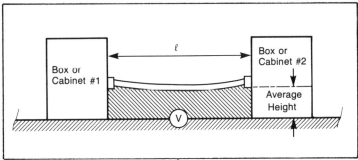

Figure B.6—Well-Defined Common-Mode Loop Area.

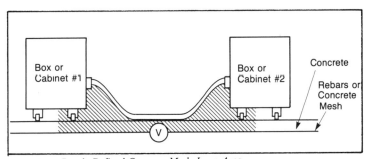

Figure B.7—Poorly-Defined Common-Mode Loop Area.

Electric-Field Coupling into Cable/Harness

Common-mode coupling converts an electric-field strength into an open circuit voltage:

$$CMC_{dB} = 20 \log_{10} (V_i/E) \text{ dB above V per V/m} \qquad (B.3)$$

where,

$$V_i/E = 2\ell \cdot \cos\theta \cdot \sin\left(\frac{\pi h}{\lambda}\cos \alpha\right), \text{ for both h and } \ell << \lambda \qquad (B.4)$$

V_i = induced-loop voltage in volts
E = impinging electric-field strength in V/meter
h = average loop height in meters
ℓ = loop length in meters
λ = wavelength in meters
   $= 300/f_{MHz} = C/f_{Hz}$
C = velocity of propagation $= 3 \times 10^8$ m/sec
α = angle between plane of loop and direction of propagation
θ = angle between direction of ℓ and E field
$\sin(\ )$ = in units of radians

Therefore, the coefficient V_i/E allows one to quickly estimate how many volts will be induced in a circuit, give the loop size, the field frequency and amplitude.

Note that in equation B.3 the orientation of the loop vs. the field is of importance, by the $\cos \alpha$ and $\cos \theta$ terms. If α and $\theta = 90°$, the induced voltage reaches its maximum. It is assumed that the situation is *not* so unfortunate that the victim circuit would be exactly oriented for maximum induction. Rather, the general case of diagonal polarization is assumed in which $\alpha = \theta = 45°$ and $\cos \alpha = \cos \theta = 1/\sqrt{2}$. This assumption is used hereafter since the user generally does not know either α or θ which may take on any value. Thus:

$$\frac{V_i}{E} \simeq \sqrt{2} \, \ell \sin\left(\frac{\pi h}{\sqrt{2}\,\lambda}\right), \text{ for } \ell/\lambda \text{ and } h/\lambda \leq 0.5 \qquad (B.5)$$

Values of the coupling coefficient V_i/E are plotted in Fig. B.8.

The parameter value in the graphs corresponds to different loop dimensions, h and ℓ. For lower frequencies, it is noted that coupling coefficient increases with frequency at the rate of 20 dB/decade which is ex-

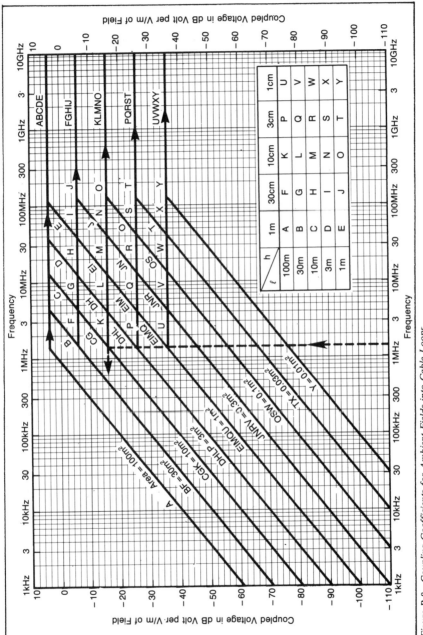

Figure B.8—Coupling Coefficients for Ambient Fields into Cable Loops.

B.7

pected from Eq. (B.7). This increase continues until the corner frequency condition of $\ell = \lambda/2$ is reached. Then coupling does not increase anymore because loop dimensions have reached those of a resonant half-wave dipole. What actually happens is that peak and nulls are *hopping* at every half-wave length. The curve has been smoothed to show the envelope of these *hops*.

Example:

A 10 m long I/O cable is installed 1 meter above ground.

The digital link has the following parameters:

- Drivers and receivers: TTL, unbalanced line receiver sensitivity: 50 mV
- Bandwidth = 10 MHz.
- PCBs have their OV grounded to chassis at both ends.
- Chassis are grounded to building ground.

An AM station located less than a mile away (see Chapter 1, section 1.2.1) creates locally, at the place the cable is installed, a field strength of 5 volts/m, at 1.5 MHz. Is there a risk of EMI? The input data are:

$$\ell = 10 \text{ m}$$
$$h = 1 \text{ m}$$
$$E \text{ field} = 5 \text{ V/m or 14 dBV/m}$$

On Fig. B.8, it can be seen that for $\ell = 10$ m and $h = 1$m, the curve to select is curve C. Locating 1.5 MHz on frequency scale, curve C is intersected at $\simeq -16$ dB.

Therefore the common-mode voltage induced in the cable vs. ground will be:

$$14 \text{ dBV/m} + (-16 \text{ dB}) = -2 \text{ dBV} = 0.8 \text{ V}$$

Since this is a CM voltage, it is not obvious that it will trigger the receiver, but since both ends are grounded, the CM rejection of the link is very poor, and 800 mV will certainly upset the 50 mV threshold of the receiver. At such a low frequency, the most immediate remedy is to change to a single point ground, i.e., to float the PCB in a piece of equipment.

Induced Voltage from Magnetic Induction

In some cases, the EMI ambient is a strong magnetic field (proximity of rotating or static inverters, powerful transformers, etc.) known by its value in Gauss, or in Amp/meter.

In that case the voltage induced is given by the derivative of the flux over the time. For worst case orientation,

(maximum flux intercept and in the air):

$$V_i \text{ volts} = \frac{\Delta\phi}{\Delta t} = -\frac{\Delta B}{\Delta t} \times \ell \times h \qquad (B.6)$$

where,
ℓ and h = loop dimensions in meters
ΔB = induction variation in Tesla (1 Tesla = 10^4 Gauss = 80.10^4 A/m)
Δt = in seconds

if the magnetic field is a sine wave,

$$V_i \text{ volts} = \omega B \times \ell \times h = 2\pi F \times B \times \ell \times h \qquad (B.7)$$

Example:

In a similar installation, as in the previous example, a strong magnetic field is created by a motor generator set located in the computer room. The magnetic field leakages have been found to be maximum on harmonic #5 (300 Hz) with an amplitude of 0.3 Gauss. Using graph B.9 it can be seen that for $\ell \times h = 10 \times 1$, one must use curve H.

At 300 Hz curve H shows 0 dBVolt per Gauss. Since 0 dBV is 1 volt, the induced voltage is:

$$V_i = 0.3 \text{ Gauss} \times 1 \text{ Volt/Gauss} = 0.3 \text{ Volts}$$

Remarks:

1) In far field (several wavelengths from radiation source), for a given electromagnetic ambient, entering E Volts/m in curve B.8 or H Amps/m in B.9 would give the same induced voltage, since E and H become related by a fixed ratio, 377 Ω.

2) To exactly measure a CM voltage, one should in fact *open* the loop and make the measurement with a high impedance device. Therefore, if the loop is closed (shorted loop) where is the voltage? It distributes, in fact, along all the impedances in the loop.

3) Although emphasis has been on the ground loop, these curves can · perfectly be used to find the voltage induced in *any* circuit loop.

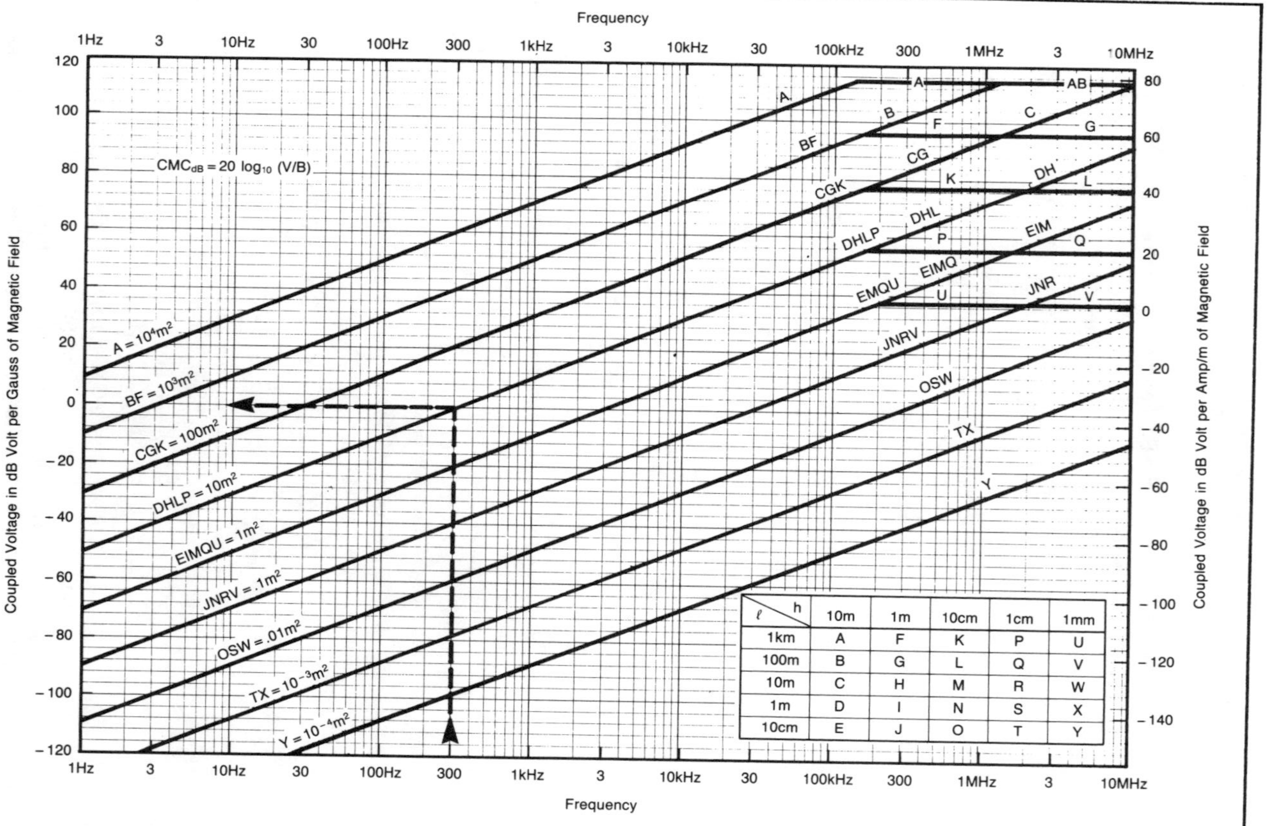

ℓ \ h	10m	1m	10cm	1cm	1mm
1km	A	F	K	P	U
100m	B	G	L	Q	V
10m	C	H	M	R	W
1m	D	I	N	S	X
10cm	E	J	O	T	Y

Figure B.9—voltage Induced by Magnetic Field into Cable-Ground Loop Area.

Appendix C
Prediction of EMI Radiation from PCBs and Digital Equipments

Background

Back when radio frequency interference was primarily a matter of radio communications transmitters and receivers, very sophisticated analytical approaches were developed to predict the interference level knowing all the parameters of the transmitting source. Then, a multitude of non-intended RF sources, producing discrete frequencies, have appeared with the proliferation of computing devices using faster and faster logic technologies to allow corresponding faster clock and bit rates. All computers and digital equipment therefore, become a threat for radio communication. A simple calculation can give an immediate feeling of the problem: assume a mini-computer consisting of a large planar board with 60 chips, each one consuming about 250 mWatts. Assuming also that only one-third of the circuits resident on these chips are toggling synchronously at an internal clock frequency of 50 MHz, for instance, it can be said that the total switched power at a given instant is:

$$1/3 \times 60 \times 0.250 = 5 \text{ watts.}$$

Now assume that a miniscule fraction of this power is *not dissipated* by Joule effect in the chips, wiring or various resistances, but is radiated instead. And assume that on the 50 MHz fundamental, only 10^{-6} of the switched power is radiated. One-millionth of 5 watts is 5 microwatts. A simple formula gives the field strength of a given radiator:

$$E \text{ volts/m} = 1/R\sqrt{30P_r} \qquad (C.1)$$

where,
  R = distance from the source in meters
  P_r = radiated power (including antenna gain)

At three (3) meters distance, the five (5) microwatts radiated from the PC board will result in:

$$E = 1/3\sqrt{30 \times 5 \times 10^{-6}} = 4 \text{mVolts/m or } 72 \text{ dB}\mu\text{V/m}$$

This is more than the minimum field strength received by TV and FM listeners in areas remote from the broadcast station. Therefore, in case of frequencies coincidence (co-channel EMI), the computer clock and its harmonics may seriously affect radio-reception in the vicinity.

The FCC and other regulatory bodies world-wide have set RF emissions limits, like FCC Docket 15J which stipulates no more than 100 μV/m (40 dBμV/m) measured at 3 m from personal computers, above 30 MHz. But to the contrary of a CW transmitter where the characteristics of the radiation source (transmitter power, antenna gain and pattern, spurious harmonics, etc.) are well identified, a digital electronic assembly is much more difficult to model. So the traditional approach is generally to design the PCB layout, mother board and interconnects using the best know-how (which, in the area of EMI may include a blend of rules-of-thumb, company's recipes and *we-do-it-this-way-because-we-always-did-it-this-way-and-it-worked*), then to run an FCC test to *see if it passes.* Needless to say (and the example above shows why), in many cases, *it does not pass,* which means re-design, E.C.'s and retrofits.

The following method allows quick prediction of radiation from printed circuits and associated wiring.

The prediction is based on solutions of Maxwell's equations for a small loop or doublet. The far field electric term from a short doublet is given by:

$$E \text{ V/m} = \frac{I \ \ell \ 60 \ \pi}{R\lambda} \tag{C.2}$$

where,
  I = current in the short wire, in Amperes
  ℓ = length of short wire in meters
  R = distance in meters
  λ = wavelength in meters

Since the radiating circuit is made of two wires more or less parallel carrying opposite currents, the net field would be null if they were infinitely close, but in fact, their separation S creates a phase difference, therefore, a non-null net field. Taking into account this phase shift gives the radiated far-field expression for a pair of parallel wires:

$$E \text{ V/m} = \left(\frac{I\ell \ 60 \ \pi}{R\lambda} \right) \left(\frac{\sin 2 \ \pi S}{\lambda} \right)$$

$$\cong \frac{I\ell \ 120 \ \pi^2}{R} \left(\frac{S}{\lambda^2} \right) \tag{C.3}$$

Since the sine of a small value approximates this value itself.

Given that $\lambda m = 300/F$ (MHz), replacing $\ell \times s$ by the area of the circuit, and using more convenient units results in:

$$E\mu V/m = 1.3 \times A \times I/R \times (F)^2 \qquad (C.4)$$

where:
    A = area of the radiating circuit in cm^2
    F = frequency in MHz
    I   = circuit current in Amps

Interestingly, the result is the same whenever we use a loop or two parallel wires.

However, these equations are based on current, which is generally not what the designer uses the most. It is often more convenient to use the drive voltage. When I is replaced by V/Z in equations, the following expression results which gives directly the radiated field as a function of the driving voltage:

$$E\mu V/m = \frac{1.3 \ A \ V \ (F)^2}{RZ} \qquad (C.5)$$

The curve in Fig. C.1 gives the field strength radiated at three meters from a circuit normalized as a 1 cm^2 loop area, driven by 1 volt, terminated by loads from 10 ohms to 377 ohms. Above the far-field transition, if loads are larger than 377 Ω, the field becomes essentially of a voltage-driven dipole, i.e., it relates to the driving voltage only. What remains to be done is to compute (or measure) the Fourier series of the digital signal.

The results are fairly accurate as long as the radiating element is electrically short $(\ell < \lambda)$. Above this, limitations are:

- at highest frequencies where the longest PCB trace exceeds $\lambda/4$, the geometry of the loop entered in the model must be clamped to $\lambda/4$ of the frequency used in calculation.

- above the same boundary, the load impedance has to be replaced by the characteristic impedance of the PCB traces.

The radiating loops can consist of (see Fig. C.2):

- The + Vdc and return traces from the power buses to the chip. In this case, the radiation is caused by the logic transition (see Fig. C.2a).

- The chip and socket leads (see Fig. C.2b).

- The signal run between chips, the path being closed via the corresponding 0 volt return trace. This is one of the most critical radiating loops since, in some cards, it can represent a significant part of the card perimeter. In Fig. C.2a, for instance, the run EFGH reveals a very large loop.

- The signal and return wires in a flat cable, etc. If the PCB is multi-layer or double-sided with ground plane, an immediate reduction of the radiating loop occurs since the spacing S now is merely the height of the traces above the ground plane (see Fig. C.2c).

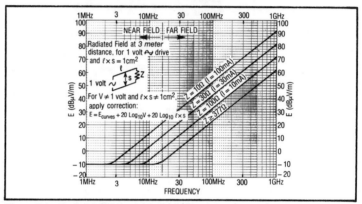

Figure C.1—Radiated Field at 3 Meters Distance from a 1 cm² Loop.

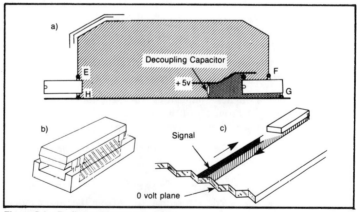

Figure C.2—Radiating Elements in PCBs.

(a) Radiating loop formed by supply traces (between the decoupling capacitor and the chip), and by signal trace and its return.

(b) Radiating loop formed by the chip and socket leads; with 50 chips or more of a PC board, the sum of these small areas can represent up to 30-50 cm², a non-negligible contribution to total radiation!

(c) The radiating loop is immediately reduced when the current can flow in a ground plane just under the trace.

Following is a practical example showing the use of the method.

Example: Radiation vs. a FCC Class B Test (3 meters distance)

Using the same digital pulses as the example in Appendix A, the radiated emission is estimated from the large card (mother board) shown in Fig. C.3. The critical (radiating) portion of the circuit consists of:

- 5 clock traces and their returns, carrying 10 MHz clock

- Voltage swing: 4 volts

- Rise time τ_r: 10 ns

- Load: 500 Ω (corresponds roughly to a TTL input with 10 pF of capacitance)

- Trace run: $\ell = 40$ cm

- Pair separations: S = 2.5 cm

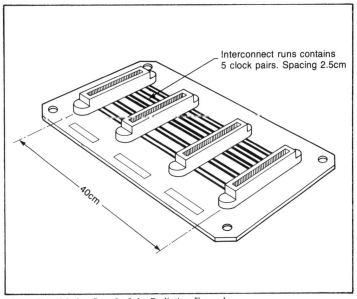

Interconnect runs contains 5 clock pairs. Spacing 2.5cm

40cm

Figure C.3—Mother Board of the Radiation Example.

Use the same form at the bottom of Fig. C.4. The amplitude of each harmonic has already been calculated in the example of Appendix A since the curves, C.1 are normalized for 1 volt, 1 loop and 1 cm², the following correction dB factors must be applied:

- the actual voltages, in dB Volt
- the area of one loop = 20 log $\ell \times$ s cm²
- the number of synchronous loops = 20 log N

One should remember that when the largest dimension ℓ reaches $\lambda/4$, the value entered in the area correction must be clamped to the $\lambda/4$ of each harmonic used in the calculation. In this case, 40 cm represents $\lambda/4$ for F = $1/4 \times 300$ MHz/0.4 m = 188 MHz. Therefore beyond 188 MHz (harmonic #18) each step shows a gradually reducing value for the effective area: the efficiency of the antenna decreases, as does the voltage spectrum. As a result the total radiation profile collapses.

The prediction indicates clearly that the FCC limit is violated by 14 dB, i.e., action has to be taken to reduce the traces loop, use a ground plane or shield the equipment housing.

By comparison, Fig. C.4 shows the actual measurements of this PCB (the tested card uses 7404 TTL inverters) on a 3-meters FCC test site. For sake of precision, it must be remarked that:

- The Fourier series gives peak value for each harmonic while the EMI receiver is scaled in RMS, which means -3 dB difference.

- The FCC procedure calls for scanning antenna height to search for maximum reading, which means up to $+6$ dB add-up when the ground reflected wave arrives in phase with the direct one.

- In an actual equipment, the radiation from common mode currents leaking by the external cables (I/Os, etc.) may be a significant contributor to the total radiation.

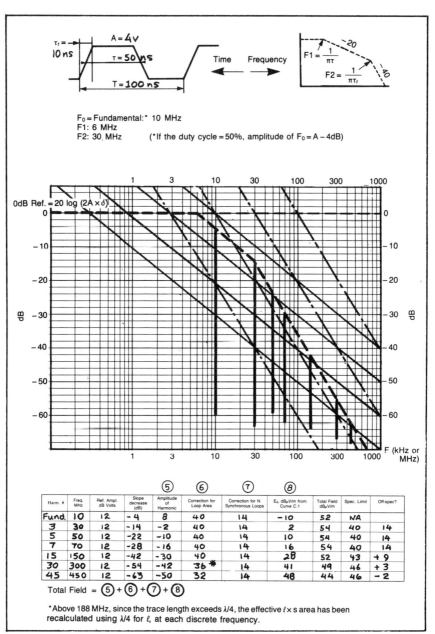

$\tau_r = 10\ ns$ $A = 4\ v$ $\tau = 50\ ns$ Time Frequency $F1 = \dfrac{1}{\pi\tau}$ -20

$T = 100\ ns$ $F2 = \dfrac{1}{\pi\tau_r}$ 40

F_0 = Fundamental:* 10 MHz
F1: 6 MHz
F2: 30 MHz   (*If the duty cycle = 50%, amplitude of $F_0 = A - 4dB$)

0dB Ref. = 20 log (2A × δ)

dB

F (kHz or MHz)

Harm. #	Freq. MHz	Ref. Ampl. dB Volts	Slope decrease (dB)	Amplitude of Harmonic ⑤	Correction for Loop Area ⑥	Correction for N Synchronous Loops ⑦	E_0, dBμV/m from Curve C.1 ⑧	Total Field dBμV/m	Spec. Limit	Off-spec?
Fund.	10	12	-4	8	40	14	-10	52	NA	
3	30	12	-14	-2	40	14	2	54	40	14
5	50	12	-22	-10	40	14	10	54	40	14
7	70	12	-28	-16	40	14	16	54	40	14
15	150	12	-42	-30	40	14	28	52	43	+9
30	300	12	-54	-42	36 *	14	41	49	46	+3
45	450	12	-63	-50	32	14	48	44	46	-2

Total Field = ⑤ + ⑥ + ⑦ + ⑧

*Above 188 MHz, since the trace length exceeds λ/4, the effective ℓ × s area has been recalculated using λ/4 for ℓ, at each discrete frequency.

Figure C.4—Radiation Prediction Form.

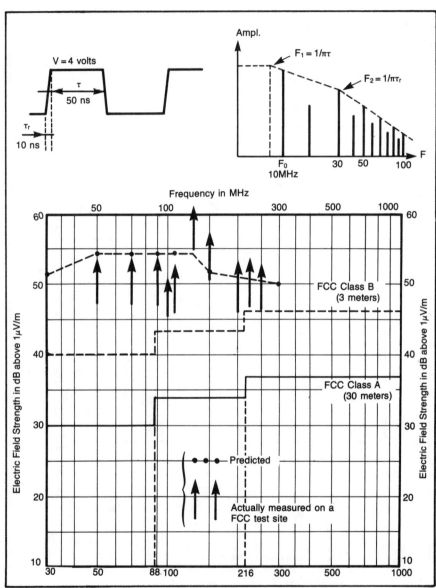

Figure C.5—Predicted vs. Measured Radiated Field from a Large PCB with 10 MHz Clock.

C.8

Computers and Digital Devices: Various Radiating Sources or Contributors

So far, radiation from PCBs has been emphasized. Is this to say that they are the most important? Certainly not. Although the PCB contains the real culprits, i.e., the chips, many paths are used by HF to *escape* from the equipment. Figure C.6 shows a conceptual view of the problem.

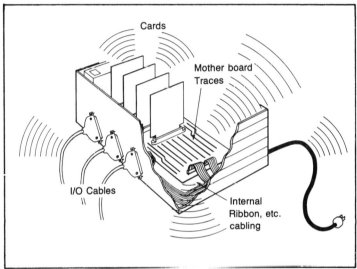

Figure C.6—The Many Radiators in Digital Equipment.

More insight is needed to understand why I/O cables and even the power cord radiate clock harmonics. Figure C.7A shows what might *normally* be expected. After all, power cord carries 60 or 50 Hz and I/O cables generally carry a slow or medium speed interface, like RS 232 with 10 kHz or 100 kHz data rate. None of these are capable of generating radiations at hundreds of MHz!

Figure C.7B shows what *actually* happens, due to facts which are not apparent to the designer, nor shown on the normal circuit diagrams. The system shown has now many radiating loops carrying stray common-mode currents. Whereas, in the PCB, there were a few ten or 100 cm^2 loops, now there are radiating loop *antennas* representing several square meters.

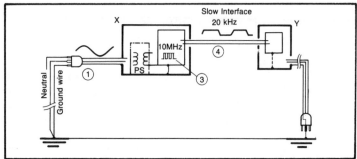

Figure C.7—a) What One Might Normally Expect: ① *power line carries only 60 or 50 Hz current.* ④ *I/O cable carries only slow interface.* ③ *10 MHz clock is contained within the electronic box.*

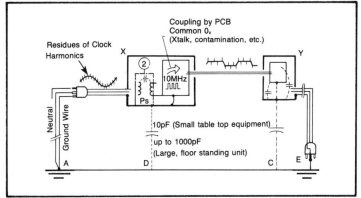

Figure C.7—b) What Real Life Provides!
—*Because of primary-to-secondary capacitance in* ② *(30 to 1000 pF in ordinary unshielded transformers) power lines and ground wires are polluted by 10 MHz harmonics.*
—*Ribbon or multipairs cables now also carry 10 MHz harmonics picked-up by internal couplings.*
—*Radiation loop can be XYCD, XYEF or combinations of both.*

This question of the common-mode excitation of external cables/ground loops is one of the most overlooked in computers noise emission. To give an example of its seriousness, Fig. C.8 shows the amount of common-mode current *injected* in the ground loop when driving a gage AWG #22 (0.66 mm) I/O pair by a 1 MHz TTL signal. Two configurations are displayed: single-point grounded (the *common sense* ground where the 0V is grounded only at the source box and ground plane) and the two ends grounded (the *no-no* of the traditional telecommunication/electronic EMC recipes). Below ≃ 30 MHz it is clear that floating one of the PCB or chassis gives a definite advantage. Above this frequency, the common-mode current circulates in the ground loop what ever circuit #2 is grounded or floated. This is not that the *recipe* was wrong. A point was simply reached where floating cannot help any more.

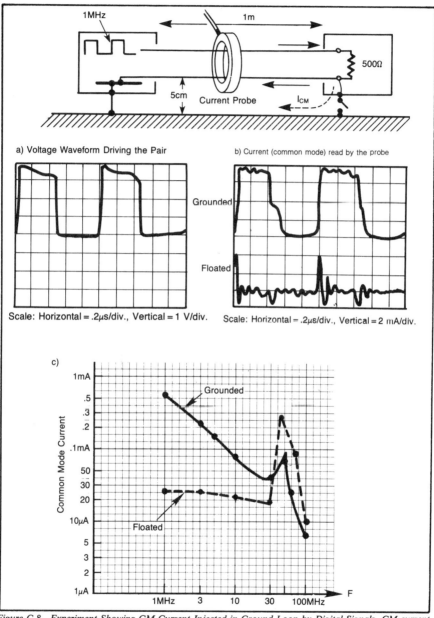

a) Voltage Waveform Driving the Pair

b) Current (common mode) read by the probe

Grounded

Floated

Scale: Horizontal = .2μs/div., Vertical = 1 V/div.

Scale: Horizontal = .2μs/div., Vertical = 2 mA/div.

Figure C.8—Experiment Showing CM Current Injected in Ground Loop by Digital Signals. CM current is measured by a clamp-on probe. If the current was purely differential, the probe should not read anything, therefore, what the probe sees is the leakage to ground. Figure b is a scope waveform of CM current, and Figure c is the same view on a frequency plot (spectrum analyzer).

It can be seen that, with a floated configuration, the peak CM current is $\simeq .3$ mA around 40 MHz where highest CM harmonics exist. By contrast, the total normal line current when driving a 500 Ω load by 4 V should be: 4V/500 Ω = 8 mA. That is, in total energy, the bulk of the pulse current is flowing back by the signal return wire (the *honest* path). But a small percentage corresponding the the sharp rise/fall times circulates in the ground loop. This leakage may seem relatively small, but one must remember the huge size of this radiating loop.

Such radiation can be predicted by the same approach used for PCBs, as long as the designer knows:

- The common mode currents (they can be measured with a clamp-on current probe) or,

- the wire-to-ground voltage and the leakage impedances (mainly capacitances).

The best method, to avoid fighting with unnecessary common-mode currents on external cables, is to keep these cables from being contaminated *from the inside* by:

- proper PCB layout, traces separation (Chap. 2)

- attention to cable families (Chap. 5)

- efficient power supply decoupling/filtering

- efficient I/O ports decoupling (Chap. 6).

References

1. White, D.R.J., *EMI Control Methodology and Procedures,* DWCI, Gainesville, Virginia
2. Keenan, R.K., *Digital Design for Interference Specifications*
3. Nakauchi, E. and L. Brashear, *Technique for controlling radiated EMI due to common-mode noise,* Proc. IEEE/EMC Symposium, September 1982.
4. Cowdell, R., *Simple Equations Compute Radiated Emissions,* IEEE/EMC Symposium, August 1983.

Appendix D
Crosstalk Between Wires and Cables

Inherited from telephony, where it addresses the parasitic coupling from one voice channel to an adjacent one, the term CROSSTALK is employed to characterize, more generally, the percentage of a signal which is coupled from a circuit #1 to a nearby circuit #2 by wire-to-wire influence. Sometimes its meaning has degenerated and, outside the EMC community, some authors use it to cover any kind of undesired noise generation within a limited area, whether it is real wire-to-wire coupling, common impedance coupling or mismatch reflections.

In this appendix, crosstalk is discussed strictly in the significance of this term, i.e., the capacitive or inductive transfer between adjacent wires.

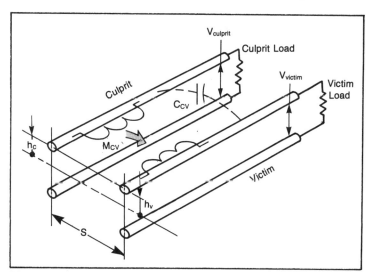

Figure D.1—Schematic View of Crosstalk.

At the risk of oversimplifying, the crosstalk problem can be represented by Fig. D.1. Two circuits that are identified as *culprit* and *victim* are running parallel over some length. As long as the circuit is electrically short, i.e., the wire length is $<<\lambda/4$ of the culprit frequency or, more precisely, the *rise time τ_r of the culprit signal* is longer than the line propagation delay τ_d, the distributed wire-to-wire capacitance and mutual inductance can be replaced by a localized capacitance C_{cv} and a localized mutual inductance M_{cv}.

Then it appears that the parasitic voltage V_v transferred to the victim by culprit line voltage V_c has two contributors:

- The capacitive coupling
- The mutual inductance coupling

If crosstalk is defined as being the ratio of $V_{victim}/V_{culprit}$, *there is a figure of merit of any given configuration, i.e., how much voltage appears on victim load per volt on the culprit line.* Since the telecommunications and EMC communities use the decibel exclusively, the Xtalk will then be:

$$\text{Xtalk} = 20 \ \log_{10} \ \frac{V_{victim}}{V_{culprit}} \qquad (D.1)$$

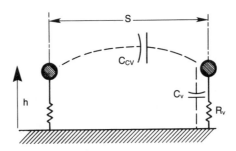

For the capacitive contributor, a crude expression of the coupling is:

$$\text{Xtalk (cap)} = 20 \ \log \ \frac{Z_v}{Z_v + \dfrac{1}{jC_{cv}\omega}} \qquad (D.2)$$

with:
Z_v = total victim impedance, including wire to ground (or return plane) capacitance C_v, and parallel combination R_v of source and load resistances.

At frequencies such as $1/C_{cv}\omega >> R_{victim}$, the capacitive crosstalk simplifies as:

$$\text{Xtalk (cap)} = 20 \ \log \ R_{victim} \times C_{cv}\omega \qquad (D.3)$$

$$\text{or Xtalk (cap)} = 20 \ \log \ 2\pi f \times R_{victim} \times C_{cv}$$

If one prefers time domain to frequency domain, the voltage induced in the victim trace can also be expressed as:

$$V_{victim} = R_{victim} \times C_{cv} \times \frac{\Delta V}{\tau_r} \qquad (D.4)$$

where, ΔV is the culprit volage swing and τ_r its rise time—with C_{cv} in Farads, τ_r in sec, or C_{cv} in nanofarads, and τ_r in nanosec.

From Eq. (D.3), it is obvious that crosstalk is a phenomenon which increases monotonically with frequency. At the worst, crosstalk could reach 0 dB, i.e., the peak voltage in victim equals the peak culprit voltage (Fig. D.2). If the frequency where $R_{vict} \times C_v \omega = 1$ occurs before the 0 dB asymptote, the crosstalk remains *clamped* to a value equal to the capacitive divider $C_{cv}/(C_{cv} + C_v)$.

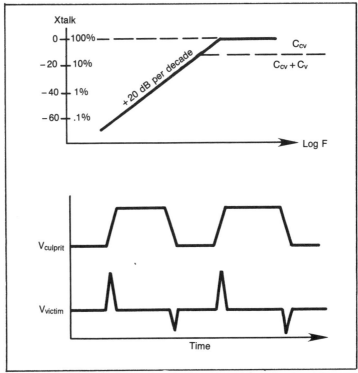

Figure D.2—Frequency and Time Domain Illustration of Capactive Crosstalk.

For the mutual inductance contributor, the voltage induced *longitudinally* in the victim is

$$V_v = M_{cv}\omega I_{culprit} = M_{cv}\omega \frac{V_c}{Z_c} \tag{D.5}$$

So the inductive contributor expresses as:

$$Xtalk_{(ind)} = \frac{M_{cv}\omega}{Z_c}$$

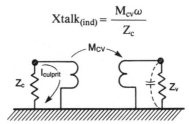

Here again it is a coupling increasing with frequency. In theory, there is no reason why the inductive crosstalk should not become greater than 0 dB, i.e., the victim induced voltage being larger than the culprit line voltage, like in a step-up transformer. However, in typical configurations, the two circuits are sufficiently similar and, being *one-turn* coupled loops, the coupling factor never exceeds unity.

It is apparent that the real contributing parameter is the culprit current which will induce the magnetic flux in the victim loop. Therefore, the determining factor is the culprit total impedance which includes the wire inductance resistance, the culprit source and load resistances *in series*.

Since we know that 2 contributors participate in crosstalk, it seems necessary to compute them separately, then retain the larger of the two, or their combination.

A look at equations (D.3) and (D.6) shows that for a given geometry, *capacitive crosstalk increases with large victim impedances,* and *inductive crosstalk increases with low culprit impedances.* The take-over of capacitive coupling over the inductive one occurs for circuit loads $\simeq 100\Omega$ (very exactly when loading equals Z_0 of the line).

So, for very high victim impedances ($Z_v >> 100\ \Omega$) the risk of crosstalk is mainly capacitive, while very low culprit impedances ($Z << 100\ \Omega$) will enhance inductive coupling.

Figures D.3 and D.4 provides a basis for computing the crosstalk between two parallel wires of AWG #22 with a sufficient accuracy (0.66 mm diam). Please note that:

- Graphs have been computed (and validated) for 1 meter of common length. Different lengths will require proportional corrections.

- Values are given for culprit and victim circuits terminated in 100 Ω at both ends. Different impedances will require corrections.

- Wires inductances and capacitances to ground have been taken into account.

- Wire diameters different than AWG #22 will cause different results. However, as long as wire diameter (including insulation) is $< S/2$, the difference is negligible.

Use the following procedure in using graphs D.3 and D.4.

- Enter the frequency of EMI voltage carried by culprit line. If EMI is a transient with rise time τ_r, enter the frequency $F = 1/\pi\tau_r$, with F in kHz for τ_r in milliseconds, or F in MHz for τ_r in microseconds, etc. (In fact, this corresponds to entering the bandwidth equivalent to the rise time).

- Select (or interpolate) wire separation S, in mm.

- Identify and select the height (hmm) of the wires above their ground plane. If the return is not a plane but another conductor such as a wire pair, enter half the height of the wire pair as shown in Fig. D.1.

If $h_{culprit} \neq h_{victim}$, use $h = \sqrt{h_c \times h_v}$.

- Look up (or interpolate) applicable crosstalk in dB for:

$$X_{cap} = \text{capacitive coupling}$$
$$X_{ind} = \text{inductive coupling}$$

- Correct for impedance and common wire length:

$$X_{cap} = X_{cap} \text{ from curves} + 20 \log_{10}\left(\frac{Z_v}{100} \times \ell_{meters}\right)$$

$$X_{ind} - X_{ind} \text{ from curves} + 20 \log_{10}\left(\frac{100}{Z_c} \times \ell_{meters}\right)$$

- Select larger of X_{cap} or X_{ind}.

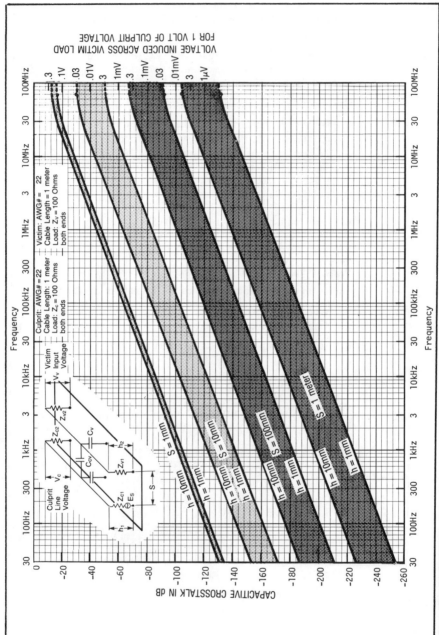

Figure D.3—Capacitive Cable-to-Cable Coupling.

D.6

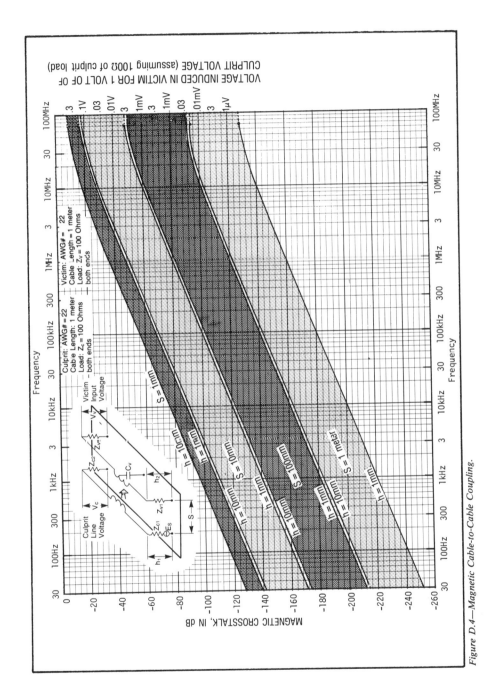

Figure D.4—Magnetic Cable-to-Cable Coupling.

D.7

The following example illustrates the use of the crosstalk prediction method:

A Schottky TTL signal is carried on a large wire-wrapped backplane. Two wires run parallel over a length of 40 cm. The parameters are:

- Culprit-victim separation: $S \approx 1$ mm

- Height above board ground plane: $h = 1$ mm

- Amplitude = 3.5 volts

- Rise time = 3 ns. Corresponds to $F = \dfrac{1}{\pi \cdot 3.10^{-9}} \approx 100$ MHz

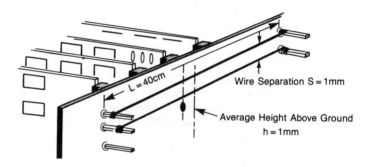

L = 40cm   Wire Separation S = 1mm

Average Height Above Ground
h = 1mm

To avoid reflections and ringing, both culprit and victim lines have been terminated by 150 Ω resistors at each end.

Inductive and capacitive coupling will be computed separately since it is not possible, a priori, to decide which one predominates.

CAPACITIVE CROSSTALK AT 100 MHz	INDUCTIVE CROSSTALK AT 100 MHz
$X_{cap} = -16\text{ dB} + 20 \log\left(\dfrac{150}{100} \times 0.40 \text{ m}\right)$	$X_{ind} = -15\text{dB} + 20 \log\left(\dfrac{100}{150} \times 0.40 \text{ m}\right)$
from curve D.3	from curve D.4
≈ -20 dB	≈ -27 dB

The larger (the less negative) is the capacitive crosstalk. Now compute the corresponding victim voltage:

$$-20 \text{ dB corresponds to } 0.1 \text{ times}$$
$$V_{victim} = 3.5 \text{ volts} \times 0.1 = 350 \text{ mV}$$

This is almost equal to the noise margin for TTL logic and is therefore unacceptable.

A few questions are in order at this time:

Q: The capacitive was selected because it was larger. However, can the magnetic crosstalk, only 7 dB below, really be neglected?

A: For a rough estimate, yes. But if more accuracy is wanted, compute the actual contribution of mutual inductance: -27 dB corresponds to about 0.04 times, i.e., by magnetic induction $3.5V \times 0.04$ or 140 mV will be actually coupled, besides the capacitive effect. Can they be simply added? Yes and no; the particularity of inductive coupling is to be in series in the victim line, while capacitive is across the line. Therefore, in the example, at the load side (far end) inductive coupling is in opposite phase from capacitive, causing an actual noise of $= 350$ mV $- 140$ mV $= 210$ mV while at the source (near end), inductive coupling has the same polarity as capacitive, causing a noise of: 350 mV $+ 140 = 490$ mV.

Q: Can one be sure that the logic circuit at victim end will react to such a transient?

A: It depends on its noise margin, i.e., its speed (see section 2.1.2). But if the culprit and victim logics are of the same type, their speeds are compatible and the victim will react to a 3 ns pulse of 490 mV.

Q: It has been said that the length should be limited to $\lambda/4$. At 100 MHz, $\lambda/4 = 0.75$ m. Are the boundaries violated by picking a 100 MHz coupling off a 1 meter length?

A: No. The curves are *normalized* to 1 meter length as a reference. In fact, above 75 MHz, they are shown by dotted line. By properly correcting the length, crosstalk was derived for 0.40 m, which is interior to the $\lambda/4$ clamp.

Q: What happens if victim and culprit impedances are very dissimilar at each end?

A: a) *For inductive crosstalk,* the culprit current is governed by culprit load impedance and wire impedance, since the crosstalk has been given in function of culprit *line* voltage, *NOT open source voltage.* If *victim* impedances are dissimilar, the voltage at victim's load will be given by this correction:

$$\text{Curve value} = 20 \log_{10} \frac{2 \times Z_v \text{ load}}{Z_v \text{ load} + Z_v \text{ source}}$$

b) *For capacitive crosstalk,* the victim voltage across the load depends on the combination of Z_v load$//Z_v$ source.

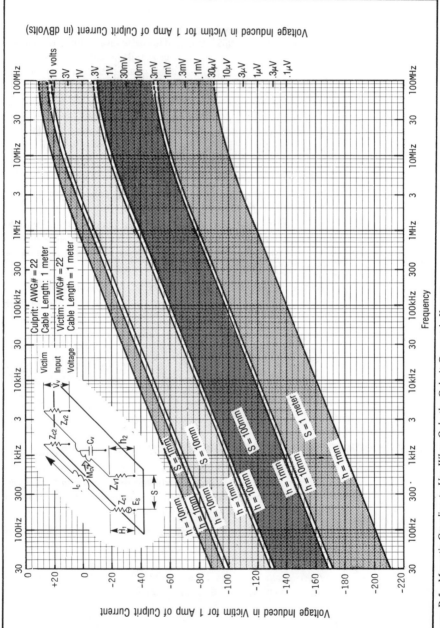

Figure D.5—Magnetic Coupling to Use When Only the Culprit Current is Known.

D.10

Another complication arises if terminating impedances are very dissimilar, and especially if they are very different from the line characteristic impedance Z_0: mismatch will cause voltage or current reflections which modify the simple crosstalk process. However, provided the near-end and far-end (addition) combination of magnetic and capacitive crosstalks are accounted for, this simple method can be used up to wire lengths equal to 0.1λ. In brief, the further the resistances at each line end are departing from Z_0, the more inaccurate becomes this simplified model for line lengths which represent a significant fraction of wavelength. More details on the mechanism are given in Reference 1 at the end of Appendix D.

Q: What if wires are twisted pairs, shielded pairs or coax?

A: Coupling prediction becomes more complex and would outgrow the purpose of this manual. Excellent numerical predictions are explained in References 2 and 4. But just remember that twisting reduces the magnetic coupling but does not cancel capacitive coupling. Shielding reduces capacitive coupling, but has little effect on magnetic coupling.

Q: What should be done if culprit voltage is *common-mode,* i.e., all wires of the culprit cable carry a pulse having the same polarity vs. ground?

A: The crosstalk curves apply perfectly provided the height "h" entered is the height of the culprit and victim *cables* above ground, instead of half the wire pair spacing as in differential-mode. The victim voltage found by this approach will be, of course, a common-mode voltage.

How Geometry and Impedances Influence Crosstalk

There are a great many parameters which influence crosstalk, like conductor thickness, conductor self inductance, fringing capacitance in the air, mismatch factor in culprit and victim circuits.

Figure D.6 summarizes the circuit parameter's dependency for crosstalk.

Parameter	Crosstalk
Cable Spacing Increase	↘
Wire-to-GND (or return conductor) Height Increase	↗
Thicker Insulation, with high ε_r	↗
Z victim LARGER	↗
Z culprit SMALLER	No influence on capacitive coupling. But causes inductive coupling to increase.
Length of Parallel Run Increase*	↗

*Note: When applying length correction add-on, be sure to clamp to $\ell \leq \lambda/4$ of EMI frequency.

Figure D.6—Geometry and Impedance vs. Crosstalk.

Simple Layout Rules Can Reduce Crosstalk at No, or Moderate, Added Cost

Several simple and easy-to-remember design guidelines can end up with trouble-free packaging rather than the *wait and see if it works* strategy:

(a) Control the ratio length/separation of parallel conductors. One centimeter of parallel runs spaced by 40 mils (1 mm) can be more fatal than 10 cm runs with 1 cm separation.

(b) Preferably run the signals *above* their ground plane or return conductor rather than co-planar layout.

(c) Strictly ban parallel runs of high speed Logic (TTL, LS, ECL) with low level analog circuits.

(d) When b) and c) cannot be achieved, consider a grounded *guard* wire, or a shield between culprit and victim wiring. Coaxial cables, in this aspect, are more immune.

Apply Stop Band Rejection for Crosstalk Between Different IC Technologies

When different technologies are involved between the crosstalk source and victim, for instance ECL and TTL, or TTL and CMOS, or even analog devices, bandwidth limitation has to be checked. If the frequency F_{EMI} of the culprit is larger than the cut-off frequency F_{co} of the victim, a relaxation equal to $20 \log_{10} F_{co}/F_{EMI}$ should be applied to the computed crosstalk. In time domain terms, one should compute that same relaxation by $20 \log_{10}$ Victim rise time/Culprit rise time. This accounts for the fact that noise immunity of the victim device improves when the pulse width of the noise stimuli becomes shorter than the minimum turn-on time of this IC family. The slope of this stop-band is generally given by the gate input capacitance, i.e., 6 dB octave or 20 dB per decade.

Crosstalk from Power Cables

So far, crosstalk has been given in terms of function of culprit's *voltage,* because this provides easy comparison of capacitive and magnetic contributors, therefore giving clues on what to do to reduce the coupling.

In some case, the only parameter which is really known is the culprit *current.* Culprit voltage *and* impedance are unknown, or too tricky to obtain. This is often the case when heavy currents are carried by power wiring, running close to low-level signal cables. For this purpose, Fig. D.7 shows the voltage magnetically induced in victim per ampere of culprit current, for 1 m length. This approach is very practical when the coupling is evidently magnetic.

Example: Assume an installation where, because of building constraints, an analog sensor wiring had been run over a length of 30 meters in the same cable tray with the power wiring supplying the air-conditioning system.

A cross section of the cable arrangement is shown in Fig. D.7. Both cables are simply protected by the PVC jacket.

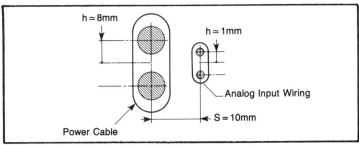

Figure D.7—Example of Magnetic Crosstalk.

During starts/stops of the air-conditioning motor, heavy inrush current of 400 Amps (10 times I nominal) occurs for a few cycles. The sensitivity of the differential analog receiver is 10 mV. Is there a risk of interference? What measures should be taken?

The average height h must be calculated to enter in the crosstalk curves:

$$h_{mean} = \sqrt{8 \text{ mm} \times 1 \text{ mm}} \approx 3 \text{ mm}$$

From Fig. D.5, pick-up a coupling coefficient for $S = 10$ mm and $h = 3$ mm (interpolation) equal to -110 dB Volts per Amp (left scale) or 3 μVolts/Amp.

So V induced $= 3\mu\text{V} \times 400 \text{ Amps} \times 30 \text{ meters} \approx 35$ mV. This is far above the threshold of the receiving amplifier.

To be on the safe side, one should reduce crosstalk by about one order of magnitude, or 20 dB; i.e., bring it down to $\leqslant -130$ dB.

To achieve this, one should either:

• increase cable-to-cable separation (curves in Fig. D.5 show that $S \geq$ about 50 mm will achieve the required objective).

• twist victim wire pair

• put the power cable in a metal conduit, not shared by the analog cable.

Conclusion

This short description does not pretend to encompass the whole subject. Tons of papers have been written on this specific matter. The bibliography on the calculation of wire-to-wire capacitance only would occupy a full shelf in a respectable library, notwithstanding that they often give different results, depending on the degree of sophistication of their mathematically or empirically derived nature.

But the user can rely on curves in Figs. D.3 and D.4 for rough prediction within 6 dB confidence, which is more than adequate in usual EMI calculations.

A good practice is to *allocate at the beginning of a design,* a certain budget for crosstalk. For instance, no more than -20 dB (10% max) of the logic immunity threshold, for each culprit-victim team.

References

1. Paul, C.R., *Prediction of Crosstalk in Wire Pairs,* IEEE EMC Transactions, Vol. EMC 21. May 1979.
2. Mohr, R.J., *Interference Coupling, Attack It Early,* EDN, July 1969.
3. DeFalco, J.A., *Predicting Crosstalk in Digital System,* Computer Design, June 1973.
4. White, D.R.J., *EMI Methodology & Procedure,* published by DWCI, Gainesville, VA 22065.
5. Ott, H.W., *Noise Reduction Techniques,* John Wiley & Son.

Appendix E
Shielding Effectiveness

Shielding effectiveness is defined as the ratio of the impinging energy to the residual energy (the part that gets through).

$$\text{For E fields} = S = 20 \text{ Log} \left(\frac{E_{in}}{E_{out}} \right) dB$$

$$\text{For H fields} = S = 20 \text{ Log} \left(\frac{H_{in}}{H_{out}} \right) dB$$

If shields were perfect, E_{out}, H_{out}, therefore P_{out} would be zero. In practice, a shield performs on 2 principles.

Absorption increases with:

- thickness
- conductivity
- permeability
- frequency

Reflection increases with:

- Surface conductivity
- wave impedance

To evaluate reflection, it is necessary to know if the shield is in near or far-field conditions. The near-field conditions are the most critical. For pure electric fields, since their wave impedance is high, it is relatively easy to get good reflection properties because the field-to-shield mismatch is large. For near magnetic fields, the wave impedance is low and it is more difficult to get good reflection.

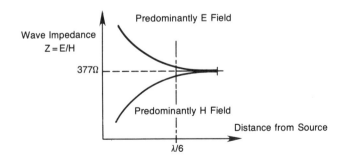

How does one know if, at distances $<<\lambda$, the field is more electric or magnetic in nature? By looking at the radiating component, one might have an idea of the predominant mode: circuits switching large currents like power-supplies, solenoid drivers, heavy current logics generate strong magnetic fields. Conversely, voltage driven high-impedance or open-ended lines create electric fields.

Like in a chain, a shield is only as good as its weakest link; therefore, it is important to know the weak points in the shields, to establish some realistic objectives.

- At low frequencies, what counts is the nature of the metal which is used: thickness, conductivity, permeability.

- At high frequencies, where any metal would provide hundreds dB of shielding, they are never seen because seams and discontinuities completely spoil the metal barrier.

A slot in a shield can be compared to a slot antenna, which, except for a 90° rotation, behaves like a dipole.

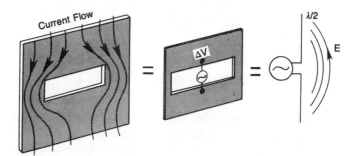

When slot length equals $\lambda/2$ the antenna is perfectly tuned, i.e., the slots in the metal barrier re-radiate if there was no shield (the only difference is that this unintentional antenna exhibits some gain and directivity). Below this $\lambda/2$ resonance, the slot leaks less and less as frequency decreases.

Figure E.2 shows some typical shielding effectiveness of conductive layers vs. frequency for the worst case conditions: a predominantly magnetic field, sourced 10 cm inside the barrier (near field conditions).

The upper curve is for aluminum or copper foil. The lower curves are for conductive paints and coatings of various surface resistances (ohms per square area). 0.1 Ω/sq. are typical of copper or zinc arc spray, while 1 Ω is representative of nickel coatings. These coatings generally have

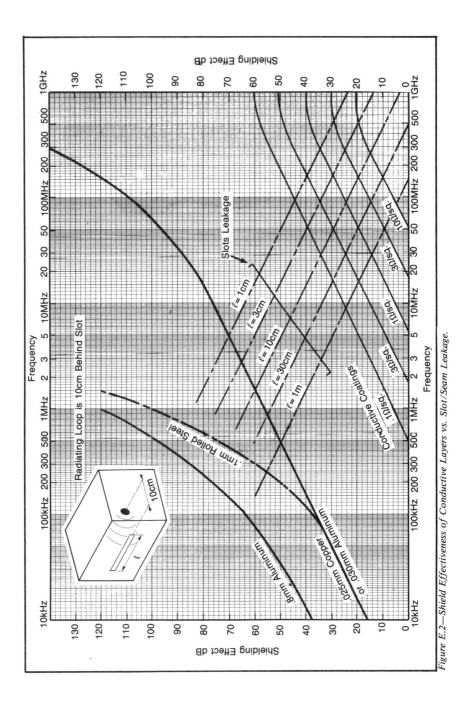

Figure E.2—Shield Effectiveness of Conductive Layers vs. Slot/Seam Leakage.

E.3

thicknesses of 30 to 50 microns and do not represent enough skin depths in the frequencies of concern (30-500 MHz) to exhibit good absorption losses. Their only chance is to provide reflection, this is why the lower surface resistances perform the best.

On the same graph are shown leakage for long slots or seams, for worst case polarization. The model is conservative in the sense that it assumes an improvement ratio like 1/F (20 dB/decade) below the $\lambda/2$ resonancy— depending on the height of the slot, actual apertures may behave differently.

How to Predict Shielding Needs

To rely *entirely* on box shielding may be a very expensive approach. On the other hand, harden the PCBs, cabling, etc. such as the unit could meet EMI specs *without any outer shield* is feasible but may also become costly. The answer is to make the best packaging possible, EMC-wise, then make-up for the remaining attenuation by the box shielding, if necessary.

Coarse Evaluation of Cabinet Design Objective

In the example of Appendix C, there was a need for the following EMI reduction:

F_{MHz}	dB Off-Spec	Safety Margin	Shielding (Rounded Up)
30	14	6	20
100	11	6	15
150	9	6	15
300	3	6	10
450	-2	6	5

Looking at Fig. E.2, it can be seen that 2 conditions are necessary:

- A box coated with aluminum foil, or with conductive paint having < .5 Ω/sq. of surface res., and

- No seam or aperture larger than 10 cm, unless they are screened or gasketed by a gasket meeting the dB requirement.

E.4

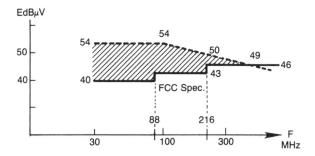

The Pragmatic Approach: Shielding Evaluation of a Prototype Cabinet

When the exactitude of the design analysis is critical, because *the cost impact in "$ per dB" is high,* the previous calculation may not be accurate enough.

A more straight forward approach is to do a real evaluation of the planned cabinet, by a substitution method. The test requires:

- A prototype of the future box with all the holes, seams, etc. as representative as possible.

- A radiating source (preferably battery operated), to avoid power cord radiation to be mistaken for shield leakage.

- An EMI receiver or spectrum analyzer and its antenna

The radiating source is located inside of the prototype box with all covers, doors, panels, etc. opened, and a first plot of the received signal at 1 or 3 meter is made.

Then all covers, etc. are closed, and secured and a new plot is made of the remaining signal. The difference in dB between the two readings is the shielding attenuation.

Appendix F
Dynamic Resistances of Digital Families

For many calculations of noise coupling (crosstalk, emission prediction, susceptibility to induced noise) a knowledge of the equivalent impedance of digital I.C.s is necessary. Although the steady state resistance is easy to find, it is not always obvious to find out what the device *looks like* during its transition time, where currents and voltages are changing non-linearly. Table F.1 based on $R_{dyn} = \Delta V / \Delta I$ gives a good approximation of the equivalent input and output impedance of digital families, during their change of state. Note also that, as for input impedance the device is always shunted by its capacitance: for instance, up to 10 MHz, a TTL gate input looks like a several kΩ resistance. Above 30 MHz, it merely looks like the 5-7 pF of its input capacitance.

Table F.1—Dynamic Resistances of Digital Families

Technology	Z_{INPUT} (Low-to-High Transit.)	Z_{OUTPUT} Low	Z_{OUTPUT} High
TTL	$$\frac{\Delta V_{in}}{\Delta I_{in}} \approx \frac{1.5v}{1.5mA} \approx 1k\Omega$$ Above $\approx 1.5v$ the device looks like a high Z, (about 10-20kΩ) without considering input capacitance. If input capacitance is considered, Zdyn $\approx$ 500 to 800Ω	$$\frac{V_{out}}{\Delta I_{out}} = \frac{0.3v}{30mA} \approx 10\Omega$$	$$\frac{\Delta v}{\Delta I} = \frac{0.8v}{5mA} \approx 150\Omega$$
LS	$$\frac{\Delta V_{in}}{\Delta I_{in}} \approx \frac{1volt}{.2mA} \approx 5k\Omega$$ (2kΩ with input cap. considered)	$$\frac{\Delta V_{out}}{\Delta I_{out}} = \frac{0.4V}{15mA} \approx 25\Omega$$	$$\frac{\Delta V}{\Delta I} = \frac{1v}{6mA} \approx 160\Omega$$
STTL Line Driver			$$\frac{1volt}{40mA} \approx 25\Omega$$
ECL	$\Delta V_{in}/\Delta I_{in} \approx 3k\Omega$	R_{out} equ.	
CMOS	$$Z_{in} = \frac{\Delta V_{in}}{\Delta I_{in}} \approx \frac{5v}{<1\mu A} \geq 5M\Omega$$ 5MΩin // with 5 pF corresponds to a dynamic impedance of $\approx$10kΩ for a 50ns rise time	300Ω (the "ON" resistance of the lower FET	300Ω (the "ON" resistance of the upper FET)

F.2

Glossary and Abbreviations

AF	audio frequency ($\simeq 0$ to 150 kHz)
AFC	automatic frequency control
AJ	anti-jamming
AM	amplitude modulation
A/M	ampere per meter (unit of magnetic field strength)
ATR	anti-transmit-receive (tube)
AWG	American Wire Gage
BB	broadband
CB	Citizen's Band
CM	common mode
CXtalk	crosstalk (parasitic coupling of one wire to another)
CMR	common-mode rejection
CW	continuous wave
dBm	dB above one milliwatt
DMC	differential-mode coupling
DVM	digital voltmeter
ECM	electronic countermeasures
EDP	electronic data processing
EED	electro-explosive device
EMC	electromagnetic compatibility
EMI	electromagnetic interference
EMP	electromagnetic pulse
EMS	electromagnetic susceptibility
ESD	electrostatic discharge
ERP	effective radiated power
FIM	field intensity meter
FM	frequency modulation
HAM	amateur radio
IBW	impulse bandwidth
IF	intermediate frequency
INR	interference-to-noise ratio
ISM	industrial scientific, and medical (equipment)
LF	low frequency (30 kHz to 300 kHz)
LISN	line impedance stabilization network
ℓ_{ne}	natural (or Neperian) logarithm
LO	local oscillator
NB	narrowband
NF	noise figure
OD	outside dimension
PAM	pulse amplitude modulation

PC	printed circuit
PCM	pulse-cross modulation
PRF	pulse repetition frequency
PRR	pulse repetition rate (same as PRF)
PWM	pulse width modulation (same as PDM)
Q	Q-Factor (f_o/BW at 3 dB points)
QP	quasi-peak
RADHAZ	radiation hazard
RE	radiated emission
RF	radio frequency
RFI	radio-frequency interference
rms	root mean square
RX	receiver
SE	shielding effectiveness. In dB, SE = 20 Log_{10} (field before shielding/field after shielding)
S/N	signal-to-noise ratio
SNR	signal-to-noise ratio
SSB	single sideband (modulation); same as SSB-SC
SSB-SC	single sideband, suppressed carrier
SWR	standing wave ratio (cf. VSWR)
SAE	Society of Automotive Engineers
TE	transverse electric (field)
TEM	transverse electromagnetic (dominant field)
TM	transverse magnetic (field)
τ_r	Rise time of a pulse (generally given between 10%-90%)
TX	transmitter
UHF	ultra-high frequency (300 MHz to 3 GHz)
ULF	ultra-low frequency (300 Hz to 3 kHz)
VCO	voltage-controlled oscillator
VHF	very-high frequency (30 MHz to 300 MHz)
VLF	very low frequency (3 kHz to 30 kHz)
VSWR	voltage standing wave ratio
VTVM	vacuum-tube voltmeter

Short List of EMC References and Bibliography

1) On EMC in General

- White, D.R.J., *EMI Control Methods and Techniques,* Vol. 3, (Don White Consultants, Inc., Gainesville, Virginia).

- Smith, Albert A. Jr., *Coupling of External Fields to Transmission Lines,* (Wiley Interscience).

- Ott, Henry W., *Noise Reduction Techniques in Electronic Systems,* (Wiley Interscience).

- Golde, R.H., *Lightning Protection,* (Chemical Publishing Co., New York, New York).

- White, D.R.J., *EMI Control Methodology and Procedures,* (Don White Consultants, Inc., Gainesville, Virginia).

2) On PCB and Hardware Design

- White, D.R.J., *EMC in Printed Circuit Boards,* (Don White Consultants, Inc., Gainesville, Virginia).

- *MECL System Design Handbook,* Motorola Technical Information Center.

- Keenan, R. Kenneth, *Digital Design for Interference Specifications,* (TKC Corporation, Vienna, Virginia).

- White, D.R.J., *Electronic Shielding Materials,* (Don White Consultants, Inc., Gainesville, Virginia).

3) On EMI Standards & Test Methods

- CISPR Publications 11, 14 and 16, (CISPR Central Office, rue de Varembe, Geneva, Switzerland).

- FCC *Rules and Regulations Vol. 2,* Parts 15 and 18, (FCC, Washington, D.C. 20554).

- VDE 871 and 875, (VDE, Merianstrasse 28, D 6050 Offenbach, West Germany).